GOAT ISLAND
AND THE U.S. NAVAL
TORPEDO STATION

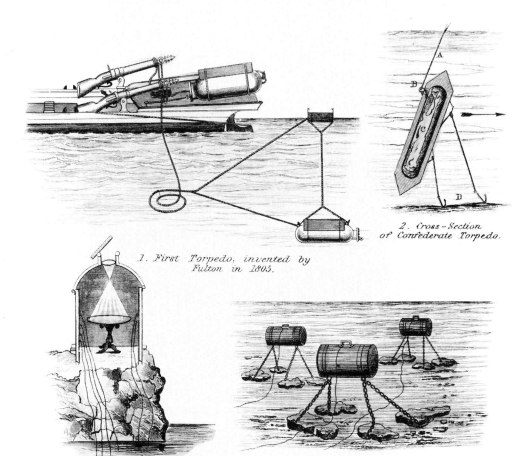

2. Cross-Section
of Confederate Torpedo.

1. First Torpedo, invented by
Fulton in 1805.

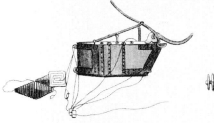

3 & 4. Gun Cotton Electric Torpedo designed
for the defence of Venice in 1859.

5. Harvey's Torpedo.

6. Whitehead Locomotive Torpedo
Woolwich Pattern.

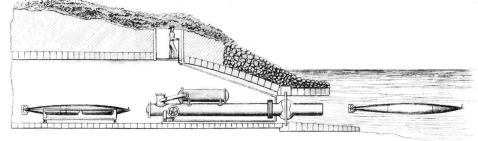

7. Whitehead Torpedo Fort.

GOAT ISLAND
AND THE U.S. NAVAL TORPEDO STATION

Guncotton, Smokeless Powder
and Torpedoes

Richard V. Simpson

AMERICA
THROUGH TIME®
ADDING COLOR TO AMERICAN HISTORY

Frontispiece : A tear sheet from the *c.* 1880 *Torpedoes and Torpedo Boats* technical magazine illustrating a surfeit of proposed and operational mines and torpedoes.

AMERICA THROUGH TIME® is an imprint of
Fonthill Media LLC
www.fonthillmedia.com
office@fonthillmedia.com

First published 2016

Copyright © Richard V. Simpson 2016

ISBN 978-1-63499-013-4

Distributed in the United States of America by Arcadia Publishing
by arrangement with Fonthill Media LLC.

For all general information, please contact Arcadia Publishing
Telephone: 843-853-2070
Fax: 843-853-0044
E-mail: sales@arcadiapublishing.com
For customer service and orders:
Toll-Free 1-888-313-2665

Visit us on the internet at www.arcadiapublishing.com

Typeset in 10.5pt on 13pt MinionPro
Printed and bound in England

This history of the U.S. Navy's first torpedo manufacturing facility is dedicated to the memory of Bristol, Rhode Island native, Rear Admiral Lucien Capone, Jr., (U.S.N.). Admiral Capone reviewed the manuscript and pronounced it historically accurate. He encouraged its publication and urged me to pursue my efforts toward that end.

Loading a Mk 14 torpedo into a unknown U.S. Second World War submarine.

Author's Note

This book is the result of 20-years research conducted for *Building the Mosquito Fleet: U.S. Navy's First Torpedo Boats*, Tempus Publishing, (2001); and another 10 years of research and collecting long out of print books, nineteenth century magazine articles, scientific journals, period photographs, and picture postcards on the subject of the torpedo weapon.

Except where specific sources are cited, the two principle resources used in this book are *A Century of Progress —A History of Torpedo System Development*, Naval Undersea Warfare Center, 1998, and *A Brief History of U.S. Navy Torpedo Development*, Naval Underwater Systems Center Technical Document 54436, 1978, compiled by E. W. Jolie.

This history of the U.S. Naval Torpedo Station on Goat Island, in Newport Harbor, Rhode Island, chronicles the research, development, technology, and deployment of the torpedo from its origin up to the 1970s.

The German technical magazine *Torpedoes* published this illustration of the German Navy's operational mines and torpedoes. German to English translation by Nathanael Greene Herreshoff, III.

Left to right: Treib-Torpedo = Floating Torpedo; Harvey's Schlepp-Torpedo = Harvey's Tow-Torpedo; Auslegen von Kontakt-Torpedo's = Laying Contact Torpedoes; Chemisch wirkender Zunder des Kontankt torpedo's = Chemically activated igniter of a contact torpedo; Torpedo-Boot mit Stangentorpedo = Torpedo Boat with a Spar Torpedo; Kontakt-torpedo = contact torpedo; Angriff mit Harvey's Schlepp-Torpedo = Attack with Harvey's Tow Torpedo; Elekrisch steuerbarer Fisch-Torpedo = Electrically controlled Fish Torpedo.

Meyer's Encyclopedia, 3rd edition, was published 1874–1878. Bibliographical Institute in Leipzig; article in regard to torpedo.

Preface

The Colonization of Aquidneck Island

Goat Island, a 10-acre outcropping of land in Newport Harbor, was called *Nante Simunka* by the native Narragansett people.

In 1524, Giovanni de Verrazzano sailed up Narragansett Bay, exploring Aquidneck Island and meeting the natives who lived there. His journal praises the fertile land and its handsome, indigenous people. By 1614, Dutch navigators and trappers were exploring the island and trading with the natives.

When the Puritan preacher Roger Williams arrived at what is now Providence, in 1636, Canonicus and Miantonomi were *Sachems* (chiefs) of the peaceful, prosperous and powerful Narragansett people. The densely wooded island of *Aquednecke* (Aquidneck), later known as Rhode Island, had rich soil and a mild climate. From its position between the land of the *Soughkonnets* (Sakonnet), a branch of the Wampanoag tribe in the east, and the Narragansetts to the west, ownership of the island was disputed for generations, and generally unsettled by either tribe.

Tradition holds that a decisive battle between the Narragansett warrior Tashtassuck, grandfather of Canonicus, gave the Narragansetts control over the island previously held by the Wampanoags. The Narragansetts considered it more a hunting ground than a place to live, and only sparsely settled the land.

In 1637, when the Massachusetts Bay Colony banished the outspoken and charismatic Puritan Anne Hutchinson with her family and followers from the colony, her friends approached Roger Williams for aid in finding somewhere for them to settle. Williams met with the Narragansett *sachems* and proposed to buy the island; the price: 40 fathoms of white beads, 10 cloth coats, and 20 hoes. Hutchinson thus became is the only woman to establish a permanent settlement in colonial America.

Within a year of their arrival on Aquidneck Island, the colonists established a permanent settlement in a place called Pocasset by the natives. The Aquidneck colonists followed the example set by the settlers of Plymouth Colony by drafting and signing the Portsmouth Compact, the first of its kind swearing no allegiance to a monarch. All members of the original Pocasset government took part in transferring the Portsmouth Colony to the opposite end of the island at Newport.

The Newport Settlement

In the summer of 1639, a new government formed among the thirty-one colonists remaining at Pocasset; they changed the settlement's name to Portsmouth.

Soon after signing the agreement, the colonist Nicholas Easton with his two sons, Peter and John, left the cove at Pocasset and sailed round the north end of the island down the west side until they came to an island where they lodged. The next morning, they named it Coaster's Harbor Island. Later, they went on to what is now Newport and began building the first English house on the east side of the present Farewell Street.

As the number of settlers increased and the village's democratic form of government became sophisticated, a general desire grew to establish a state separate from all other governments. On September 19, 1642, a committee was appointed to consult to procure a patent (A decree from the sovereign authorizing a self-governing colony) for this island and adjacent lands. Roger Williams traveled to England in the summer of 1643 to solicit a patent for Providence Plantations, Newport, and Portsmouth.

In May 1647, Portsmouth, Newport, and Providence adopted the Charter of Providence Plantations. At that meeting, the colony incorporated the anchor as part of its official seal, and the council adapted the "laws of the Province of Providence Plantations in Narragansett Bay."

Welcome Arnold Greene
Providence Plantations for 250 Years

CONTENTS

An armed sailor is watching over a cluster of three torpedo tubes ready for installation on a destroyer.

Introduction

Weaker nations have always sought to augment the strength of their navies by the use of "diabolical" contrivances for destroying an invader's ships. These often took the form of fire-ships which were ignited and allowed to drift among an enemy's fleet, scattering it. Until sails gave way to steam propulsion, and iron superseded wood in the construction of warships, this method was attended with a fair degree of success. However, the march of science left this system outmoded.

The first use of the word "torpedo" was by Robert Fulton around 1800 to describe a device with an enclosed mass of gunpowder, which explodes beneath an enemy ship. The word was probably chosen due to the similarity in the way the device and the torpedo fish both communicate shock, or simply because detonation of an underwater charge renders fish torpid. In any case, the word "torpedo" was commonly applied to all underwater explosive devices through most of the nineteenth century. David Bushnell, Robert Fulton, Samuel Colt, and other early inventors were concerned with stationary torpedoes—today called mines.

Credit for the idea of providing mobility to the torpedo, thereby turning it into an offensive weapon, goes to Robert Fulton. The earliest recorded use of a torpedo (a mine) was in 1801 when Fulton, in a demonstration to the French authorities, approached a small ship in the harbor of Brest in his invention, a submersible boat called *Nautilus*. He destroyed his target using a submarine mine with an explosive charge of 20 pounds of gunpowder that he attached to the ship's underwater hull.

Colonel Samuel Colt, Hartford, Connecticut's creator of the world-famous revolver, demonstrated a static torpedo mine in New York Harbor in 1829. His device was a pioneer version of the modern observation mine—a static canister of explosive which lying submerged can be detonated by an electrical firing circuit operated from the shore as a ship passes over it. Colt's device was ingenious but it meant that the target had to steer towards the explosive device rather than the preferable alternative of having the explosive device move towards the target.

Later, during the Crimean War (1854–1856), the Imperial Russian Navy used stationary torpedoes on a large scale in defense of Sveaborg in the Baltic Sea, where torpedoes exploded beneath four British ships near Kronstadt.

During the American Civil War, in July 1862, after two shattering Confederate defeats on the same day at Vicksburg and Gettysburg, the Confederate Navy released its biggest threat to the Union Navy: the spar torpedo. A swift, small steamer manned by a suicide crew, poked their spar torpedo—actually a bomb on a long stick—against the wooden hull of their enemy, igniting the bomb with a halyard trigger. The object was to blow a hole below the vessel's waterline, sinking the enemy.

On the night of October 27, 1864, the Confederate ironclad ram, the *Albemarle* was sunk at her berth on the Roanoke River at Plymouth, North Carolina, in a surprise attack led by Union Navy Lieutenant William B. Cushing. Cushing's weapon was an explosive charge rigged to the end of a long pole projecting from the bow of a steam launch, detonated by pulling a lanyard—another form of spar torpedo. This exploit—the first successful Union sinking of an enemy vessel using an underwater explosive—made Cushing a naval hero, and several decades later, the U.S. Navy's first class of torpedo boats was named after him.

The part played by torpedoes in the American Civil War attracted worldwide attention. However, it fell to the English engineer, Robert Whitehead to push "to the limits of man's inventive powers" by creating his self-propelled "fish" torpedo a few years later. Before Whitehead produced his version of the torpedo, many other brilliant inventors, had tried and failed.

The fact that 28 ships on both sides of the Civil War conflict were lost to mines (then called torpedoes) alerted the U.S. Navy to the promise of these new weapons. While the war was still going on, plans were afoot to create an experimental station for advanced torpedo technology. In July 1869, the newly appointed Secretary of the Navy, George M. Robeson, announced the establishment of the Naval Torpedo Station (NTS) on Goat Island in Newport Harbor.

Above left: The CSS *Albermarle* prior to its destruction by Lieutenant Cushing.

Above right: In 1893 Scribner's *St. Nicholas* magazine published this illustration of the Federal Navy's ship the *New Ironsides* being destroyed by the Confederate spar torpedo boat the *David* off Charleston in 1864.

The First Naval Torpedo Station

The Navy took formal possession of Goat Island in 1869. The current Newport Laboratory's origins date back to that year with the establishment of the Naval Torpedo Station on Goat Island. Commander E. O. Matthews was designated first Commanding Officer with the title Inspector of Ordnance in Charge. Extensive experiments with guncotton led to an order from the Bureau of Ordnance in 1882 to develop and manufacture the explosive for use in guns and torpedo charges. A guncotton plant with a production capacity of 300 pounds a day was constructed in 1883. Meanwhile, nearby Rose Island was used as a storage facility for the guncotton and smokeless powder produced. Production continued until 1907.

From the Station's inception, the principal function included training, and by 1873, a course of instruction for officers in the use of torpedoes in naval warfare was established. Training in the care, handling, and operation of torpedoes and explosives followed in the early 1880s, and a seaman gunners' school became established in 1885. By 1893, the Station was deeply involved in torpedo handling equipment, launchers, and guidance devices (today referred to as fire control). In 1910, torpedo instruction separated from the gunnery school, and just prior to the First World War, the Station was providing instruction in such diverse fields as deep-sea diving, electricity, and printing.

Before and during the war Newport continued to manufacture torpedoes and train torpedo men. The Station also manufactured primers, and perfected towed and aerial bombs. In the summer of 1917, successful tests demonstrated the practicality of a depth charge bomb in combating German U-boats. Interest in harbor defense, including mines and nets, led to the manufacture and assembly of naval defense mines. The Mk 6 mine, developed by the Station during the war, was used in extensive planting operations carried out by the U.S. Navy in the North Sea. Experiments with harbor defense nets and net-cutting torpedoes continued intermittently until the Second World War.

In 1919 the Navy acquired Gould Island, another small island in lower Narragansett Bay, for the storage of torpedoes, warheads, and explosives. In 1921, two PT seaplanes were assigned to the Station for testing aerial torpedoes. From 1923 to 1939, the Newport Naval Torpedo Station was the sole manufacturer of torpedoes in the United States and the headquarters for their research, design, and overhaul. Major emphasis was put on the modernization of the in-service weapons, on methods for aerial launching, and on new-design torpedoes. The thirties saw the gradual development and modification of the Mk 13 aircraft torpedo, the Mk 14 submarine torpedo, and the Mk 15 anti-destroyer torpedo. Station funding for assembly and research grew from $63,000 in 1931 to $7.5 million in 1940, and soared to $47 million in 1943.

Torpedo production during the Second World War totaled about 17,000 with a peak output reaching 5,656 torpedoes in the crucial war year of 1944. Additionally, during the war the Station made 75,000 torpedo test firings on the range facility on Gould Island. The Mk 14 torpedo, the most widely used torpedo in the war, accounted for sinking four million tons of Japanese shipping. The Mk 13 aircraft torpedo also played an important role in the Pacific theatre. In 1945, following the surrender of Japan, the Navy stopped all torpedo manufacture at Newport. The BuOrd [the Bureau of Ordnance] declared its new mission now would include design, research, and experimental torpedo work, ranging and proofing weapons, and the storage and issue of torpedoes and component parts.

The Naval Underwater Systems Center Today

Today's Newport Laboratory of the Naval Undersea Warfare Center, with its historical beginnings as the Naval Torpedo Station, continues the work begun in 1869. Nineteenth century ordnance work in Newport focused on research, development, test and evaluation in such emerging technologies as smokeless powder, electricity, automobile torpedo propulsion, and explosive ordnance. The mission of the twenty-first century Newport Laboratory has expanded as technology has opened new horizons in the fields of propulsion, range instrumentation, fire control systems, launchers, oceanography and underwater acoustics.

Newport's Naval Torpedo Station became the Naval Underwater Ordnance Station in 1951. At the same time, the Navy Department organized the Central Torpedo Office, which, in 1953, led to the formation of the Naval Underwater Systems Engineering Center. This merged in 1966 with the reorganized Naval Underwater Ordnance Station, creating a much larger research and development facility. Four years later, that operation with its highly skilled and experienced staff of scientists and engineers, became the Newport Laboratory headquarters of the Naval Underwater Systems Center.

Beginning on the tiny 10 acre Goat Island with a plant valued at some $50,000 and with just a handful of employees, the Naval Torpedo Station has grown to occupy some 1,500 acres with real estate and equipment property value of about five hundred million dollars. Today, as the Naval Undersea Weapons Center, the laboratory employs about 135 U.S. Navy officers and more than 3,500 civilians. The Center's major laboratory occupies a former potato field at Coddington Cove in Newport; it operates major outpost detachments in Bermuda, West Palm Beach and the Bahamas.

Production Record

Date	Torpedoes	Employees
1871	1	24
1911	20	500
1920	381	3,200
1944	5,656	13,000

Goat Island and
the Continental Navy

How did Goat Island get its name? The first reference is in an official report in 1673 by a committee of the Town of Newport. It possibly acquired the name because of its green-grassed, rocky-edged land, an ideal situation to graze Goats. Goat Island lies low in the middle of Newport Harbor; Benedict Arnold, the first colonial governor of Rhode Island, and John Greene, bought it from the Indians in 1658. The price of six pounds ten shillings included two other small islands in Narragansett Bay, Coaster's Harbor Island and Dyer's Island.

When England was at War with Holland in 1664, the colony became very alarmed at the possibility of invasion by the Dutch Fleet. The colonists petitioned the London government to erect defenses in Narragansett Bay. The Crown ignored their request. This was an important lesson for the Rhode Islanders. The town of Newport then purchased the islands from Arnold and Greene in 1676, with the intention of creating their own fortifications to protect Newport's inner harbor.

During the late seventeenth century, many towns along the east coast of North America were ports of refuge for pirates. They brought their ill-gotten goods to these towns, and their armed ships lying off the defenseless coast placed the island at their mercy. Unintimidated, these ruthless sea raiders went ashore to enjoy the opportunities for debauchery. The infamous privateer turned pirate Captain William Kidd found refuge for a time in Rhode Island.

Rhode Island, especially Newport, needed a strong hand at the helm. It found that leader in Governor Samuel Cranston who served twenty-nine years as governor of the colony. One of his first acts was to issue a proclamation against pirates. However, paper proclamations without powder and shot behind them were of little value against the outlaws. The first fort built on Goat Island was financed with money raised by lottery, the Colony of Rhode Island agreeing to take 1,000 tickets.

Cranston wisely decided to build a fort in the middle of Goat Island, mounting fifteen cannons. Additionally, forty-three building lots were laid out at each end of the island. In 1695, John Hix acquired about an acre of land on the island for a shipyard. Soon, more commercial maritime enterprises were established; in 1699, a fish packing plant existed on the north end of the island.

Island Fortifications

The first earthwork fortification constructed on Goat Island in 1703, was named Fort Anne, after the reigning Queen of England. Earthwork ramparts, however, did little to make Newporters feel secure. The fort was mainly for defense against pirates; the commanding officer was to sink any vessel coming into the harbor that did not "strike" or lower its topsail.

During the eighteenth and nineteenth centuries, the whole of Rhode Island, as colony and later state, had a reputation as a pirate refuge. One early source calls Rhode Islanders a "set of lawless and piratical people." This is probably the origin of the state's nickname: Rogues Island. Pirates, calling themselves "free traders", could bring their prizes into the colony's ports for sale without fear of reprisal. The Admiralty Court in Newport was so lax that when one miscreant, unaware of the sympathetic reputation of the court, pleaded guilty to piracy, the astonished court judged they had not heard the plea correctly and acquitted the accused for lack of evidence.

Pirates

Building the fort prevented pirates from entering inner Newport Harbor, but for many years they continued to make the Rhode Island coast and its islands their anchorage. Such piratical lawlessness continued until 1723, with the fierce clash between two pirate sloops, the *Ranger* and the *Fortune,* and the British sloop-of-war H.M.S. *Greyhound.* The pirate ships were harassing friendly shipping along the coast of the southern colonies. They sailed northward in search of more profitable hunting grounds, and attacked what they thought was a rich merchant ship. It proved to be H.M.S. *Greyhound*, mounting twenty guns. One of the marauders escaped; the other was not so fortunate. The ship was captured with its surviving crew of 36 men. They were taken to Newport, tried, and 26 of them were hanged on July 19, 1723, and buried near the execution site "within the flux and reflux of the sea" at Gravelly Point. As late as 1760, four more pirates were tried in Newport, convicted, hanged at Easton's Beach, and buried between high and low water on Goat Island.

By 1738, a stone fort had replaced the island's earlier earthwork fortifications. By then the colonists had a new king, George II. Fort Anne was renamed Fort George.

By the mid-1700s, friendly relations between the Rhode Island Assembly and the Crown were souring. The British took possession of Goat Island and its fort when they arrived to occupy the colony. Newporters grew uneasy having an armed garrison controlling access to their harbor.

The Continental Navy

The first act of open resistance to British rule occurred on July 9, 1764. Crewmembers from the British revenue schooner *St. John* attempted to carry off an alleged deserter from

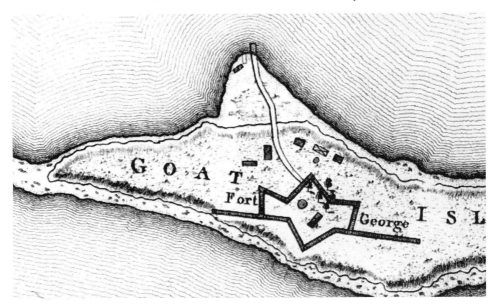

During Rhode Island's colonial days the Goat Island fortification was named Fort George, in honor of King George II; during the American Revolution the fort's name remained the same, but now honoring General George Washington.

Newport. Then the *St. John,* commanded by Lieutenant Hill, captured an American brig said to have discharged a cargo at Howland's Ferry in Tiverton without paying duties. The townspeople, angered by these high-handed acts, seized Fort George. The fort's new garrison turned their cannon upon the British frigate the *Squirrel,* firing eight shots.

Newport attacked another British ship in 1769, the armed sloop *Liberty.* This time, however, they seized the ship and scuttled it at the end of Long Wharf, off Goat Island's Gravelly Point. In 1772, Rhode Islanders, in the west bay just a few miles from the City of Providence, caught the British ship *Gaspee* and burned her to her waterline.

In 1773–1774, British engineers conducted a thorough survey of Narragansett Bay and the islands "with a view to the establishment of a very extensive Naval Station, with dry docks, ship yards, hospitals, fortifications, &c." But the approaching American Revolution ended all such British plans for developing a naval base. By the outbreak of the American Revolution Newport had reached a peak of maritime prosperity. It was the fifth most prosperous commercial center in the original thirteen colonies. Only Philadelphia, Boston, New York, and Charleston exceeded Newport in size and importance

At the beginning of the Revolution, its population was just over 11,000. The old town boasted seventeen producers of sperm oil and candles, five rope-walks, three sugar refineries, one brewery, and 22 distilleries of rum, all producing valuable commodities for the slave trade. In its foreign commerce, Newport had upwards of 200 ships employed; while its domestic trade had the services of nearly 400 coasting vessels. In June and July 1774, 64 vessels from foreign voyages registered at the Newport Custom House. In the same time 132 coasting vessels, and seventeen engaged in whaling are listed in the Custom House registry. A regular line of packet ships communicated with London. At least 3,000 sailors thronged the port, and found employment on the ships lining its docks.

Newporters' old fear of vulnerability from the sea, which had led to the purchase and fortification of Goat Island more than 100 years earlier, had come to pass. Originally the Newporters, chiefly of British stock, had feared attack by pirates, the French or the Dutch. It is ironic that a British commander, Sir Henry Clinton, led the invasion when it finally came.

The Continental Navy mounted a blockade and siege of Aquidneck Island in an effort to oust the British, which culminated in the major but inconclusive Battle of Rhode Island in 1778. This contest was the first allied effort of the Americans and their new French allies.

The combination of a Newport garrison reinforced by a large British fleet, the shelling of the French fleet from Fort George, coupled with a hurricane in April 1778 that severely damaged the French fleet, left the British still in control of Newport. Severely short of food and supplies, Clinton finally left Aquidneck one year later.

When the war ended, Aquidneck Island and Newport in particular faced unheard of devastation with the island's fresh water polluted; the city's timber wharves torn apart and burned as firewood. Business people and trading houses deserted the town for Providence or Boston. As the town's trade slowly recovered, there was an attempt to establish a naval shipbuilding yard at Newport in 1798. Although local politicians were unable to persuade the Federalist Congress to back such an enterprise, the Government did support building shipyards in Boston and Portsmouth, New Hampshire.

Harper's Weekly published this full page graphic of the Naval Torpedo Station in its February 5, 1876 edition. *From the top, down:* an electric plotting board used to detonate submerged mines. A longitudinal view west of the Torpedo Station as seen from the vicinity of Newport's Long Wharf. (*Left*) Warships deploying Harvey towing torpedoes; (*center*) a spar torpedo attack; (*right*) a Lay torpedo is seen approaching a warship. (*Bottom*) a fanciful display of assorted torpedoes.

Federal Government and Goat Island

In 1799, the town of Newport transferred ownership of Goat Island to the Federal Government for $1,500, with the express purpose of maintaining a military fort to defend Newport Harbor. The island came under the jurisdiction of the War Department, and for the following 70 years, defenses operated under the control of the U.S. Army. During the Revolution, the existing fortification was renamed Fort Liberty, later Fort Washington, in honor to General George Washington, and finally Fort Wolcott, to honor the services of Rhode Island's wartime Governor, Oliver Wolcott.

The Army abandoned Fort Wolcott in 1827. When the last company of United States Artillery stationed at the fort moved to a new post in the south, not a soldier remained on the island. The only inhabitant remaining in the fort was a civilian caretaker.

Things remained quiet in Newport until the Civil War. Fort Wolcott, along with Fort Adams, on the southwestern shore of Newport Harbor, had fallen into disrepair. On May 8, 1861, the calm of a balmy spring afternoon was shattered by the sound of heavy cannon fire. They saw the frigate *Constitution*, "Old Ironsides," her guns thundering an answer to the 24-gun salute from Fort Adams. On board were 130 midshipmen from the recently evacuated Naval Academy at Annapolis. They were supposed to go to Fort Adams, but the staff preferred to look for suitable quarters in Newport, in a nicer part of town. Until such quarters were built at Fort Wolcott, professors and ranking naval officers took temporary residence at the fashionable summer resort the Atlantic House Hotel.

A few hours later the steamer *Baltic* entered the harbor; on board were the professors, their families, and every book and piece of equipment that they could carry from the Academy. The *Constitution* was soon joined by the Naval Academy school ships the *Macedonian* and the *Santee*. These tall ships soon became a familiar part of the Newport skyline.

Naval Academy

It was no accident that the Navy chose Newport as the wartime location of the Academy. George Bancroft, who as Secretary of the Navy had founded the Academy in Annapolis in 1845, was a life-long summer resident of Newport. To Secretary Bancroft, Newport seemed the perfect wartime location for the Academy. The War Department lent Goat

During the sweltering southern summers, the elegant Atlantic House usually played host to an aristocratic southern plantation clientele. When the Naval Academy evacuated Annapolis at the start of the Civil War, ranking naval officers and others took temporary quarters at the hotel.

Island to the Navy and built temporary classrooms next to Fort Wolcott. Although there were early misgivings, native Newporters soon came around. It was not long before faculty members became involved in the Newport social scene. Many of these Newport midshipmen made names for themselves in their naval careers.

Two such early Academy graduates were Benjamin Tilley, the first military governor of Guam, and Charles V. Gridley, who at the battle of Manila was given the famous order by Admiral George Dewey, "You may fire when ready, Gridley." Rear Admiral Charles Sperry, class of 1862, later became President of the Naval War College; Sperry established the first Boy Scout troop in Newport in 1911.

Rear Admiral Stephen B. Luce

Newport also gained some important advocates in the Navy while the Academy was there. Chief among these was Rear Admiral Stephen B. Luce, who had lobbied long and hard for a naval training facility in Newport. Luce was the leading intellectual in the Navy, an individual of rare genius and ability in military and naval science. He began his career in 1841 as a midshipman aboard the 74-gun ship-of-the-line *North Carolina*, commanded by Newport native, Matthew Calbraith Perry. Twenty years later at the outbreak of the Civil War Luce demonstrated his interest in the region. At the time, he was assistant commandant of the fledging Naval Academy in Annapolis. With the conflict so close to the academy, Luce decided to move the academy elsewhere. His strong augments in favor of Newport, convinced Navy Secretary Gideon Welles, and the island site was chosen.

Before the war ended, Luce was lobbying politicians to keep the Naval Academy in Newport. His efforts failed however, and the Naval Academy returned to its original site in Maryland. However, fears that the Navy would abandon Newport altogether were quickly dispelled. Soon after the war, a series of events led to a permanent Navy presence in Newport. There is good reason to believe that Luce was primarily responsible for establishing the Torpedo Station on Goat Island. He made the decision for the site two months after President Grant took office in 1869.

The Historical Perspective to Torpedoes

Mines—known in the late 1800s as stationary torpedoes—were first employed by the Russians in the 1850s during the Crimean War, but to little effect. During the American Civil War, however, they became a deadly, albeit crude, weapon. The Confederates first introduced this form of warfare by planting torpedoes in the Savannah River in February 1862. These stationary torpedoes were anchored to the river bottom. The assumption was that vessels passing over them would entangle lines, which on being pulled would cause a friction primer to explode. Unfortunately for the Confederates, these weapons were not the success that was hoped for as they were easily found and removed by the Union forces.

About this time, in the Confederate capital Richmond, an organized Torpedo Corps was formed to perfect this new weapon. A more elaborate device was the buoyant torpedo with its accompanying so-called "devil's circumventor." Because the anchoring was stealthy, it was less likely to be discovered. In case the enemy should find it, a line attached to the primer of the circumventor would trigger its explosion with the expectation that it would cause great damage. Later, the electric fuse placed control of the weapon in the hands of an operator on shore.

These early mines could be of enormous dimensions, some containing nearly a ton of black powder. Such relatively inexpensive barrel-mine torpedoes caused the loss of the *Tecumseh* at Mobile and the *Patapsco* at Charleston.

The Confederacy was short of warships that could go up against the Union Navy's many superior ships bristling with heavy cannons. The South, forced to resort to novel devices to defend itself against the Union's powerful fleets, began building ironclad ships whose armor could withstand the explosive shells of naval guns. During the second year of the war, the Confederacy began experimenting with torpedoes as offensive weapons. The Confederate Navy employed various types of torpedoes, and enjoyed some success. Confederate torpedoes damaged twelve and sank 22 Union ships, while Union Navy torpedoes destroyed just six Confederate ships.

A period wood engraving by Robert Weile illustrating the destruction of the Federal Monitor *Tecumseh* by a Confederate spar torpedo in Mobile Bay, on August 5, 1864.

Spar Torpedoes in the Civil War

The Confederate spar torpedo boat attack against the Federal Navy's armor-plated *New Ironsides* in October 1863 was unsuccessful; the ship's iron plates survived the explosion. A spar torpedo attack on February 7, 1864 against the wooden-hulled *Housatonic*, had better results; the explosion ripped open the ship's hull, sinking her.

The first Federal effort to destroy a Confederate ship came on the night of October 27, 1863, when Lieutenant William Barker Cushing and 14 volunteers set out on their 8-mile trip up the Roanoke in their 30-foot steam launch. Cushing's target was the ironclad CSS *Albemarle*; his weapon a cumbersome canister of black powder on the end of a 16-foot spar. Cushing's launch drew close to the ship, until spotted by the *Albemarle's* crew, and under a rain of gunfire, Cushing rammed his torpedo into the ship's side below the waterline and pulled the trigger lanyard of the weapon. The explosion threw the steam launch into the air, and most of the crew tumbled into the water. The *Albemarle*, with a gaping wound in her side, slowly keeled over, crushing Cushing's launch and sinking her. Cushing and his men swam to safety under a shower of grapeshot and musket balls.

The fuses employed in spar torpedoes were percussion and exploded on contact. Seven fuses were sometimes employed for one torpedo, which was cylindrical with hemispherical ends.

The use of spar torpedoes by both Federal and Confederate navies to sink enemy ships proved ironclads were no safer from torpedo attack than wooden warships. American Civil War naval combat showed that mine (torpedo) warfare would continue to play a vital part in modern naval warfare. Until the introduction of Robert Whitehead's automobile torpedo in the 1870s, the small steam-powered launch remained an important launching platform.

The spar torpedo used by Cushing to sink the *Albemarle* suffered the disadvantage of requiring its operators to be within the spar's length to set the explosive. Thus the chances of success or even survival were slim.

This official U.S. Navy photograph illustrates a Torpedo Station spar torpedo boat rigged out for action in Newport, Harbor. The explosive charge of guncotton is fastened to the end of a spar (pole). This is secured to the launch and so rigged that it can be projected forward or abeam and lowered well below the waterline of an enemy vessel; the charge is exploded on contact or by means of a lanyard trigger.

J. A. Williams snapped this stereoscopic photo of a spar torpedo explosion in Newport Harbor *c.* 1880. *Image courtesy of Larry and Laura Rochette*

Founding
the Naval Torpedo Station

After the Civil War, when Admiral David Dixon Porter became Assistant Secretary of the Navy, he began to actively campaign for the creation of a station to conduct hands-on experiments with torpedoes, mines, explosives, and electrical devices to determine how to employ this new technology. Admiral Porter's foresight and determination were key factors in establishing the Navy's need for specialized technical activities, and he planted the seeds from which the current U.S. Navy laboratories evolved. Porter formed a committee to examine sites for the experimental station, and in July 1869, the Secretary of the Navy announced that a new activity would be located on Goat Island in Newport, Rhode Island.

Newport's modern naval history begins on July 29, 1869, when the Department of the Navy gently eased the Army off Goat Island to establish a research facility, the Naval Torpedo Station. Commander E. O. Matthews was designated the first Inspector of Ordnance in Charge [1869–1873]. The original mission for the Torpedo Station was to serve as the Navy's research and experimental center for the development of torpedoes and torpedo equipment, explosives, and electrical equipment.

The War Department placed a value of $50,000 on the island; the Navy took control for an annual payment of $5,000. Commander Matthews, after assuming his new Command, faced the formidable task of starting the Navy's first Torpedo Station. The broad mission was to function as both an experimental station and a school in a wide range of new weapon technologies including:

- Stationary torpedoes [moored mines];
- Spar and towed torpedoes including design, development, and fleet use;
- Automobile torpedoes;
- Explosives, including design, development, and production;
- Electricity and electrical devices including fuses, accumulators [batteries], lighting systems, dynamos [generators], and wire-guided torpedoes.

The Station Organization

In discussing the formation of the Naval Torpedo Station, the conventional title of "Commanding Officer" is generally used. However, the formal title of the Station's Senior Office is "Inspector of Ordnance in Charge." Staff officers could be assigned as "Inspectors of Ordnance," a formal title remaining in effect until December 1943. The Inspector of Ordnance was responsible for overseeing contract procurements including manufacturing, cost, quality, and scheduling and certifying that all items met required specifications, and verifying performance. Additionally, he was responsible for the fleet introduction of new items including training, providing special support equipment (the ordnance outfit), certifying that the ship was proficient in operating the ordnance, and conducting periodic inspections to check the ship's company. Most Inspectors of Ordnance were lieutenants and the breadth and depth of their responsibilities, professional dedication, and expertise was impressive. Eventually, a huge bureaucracy evolved to manage the staggering number of tasks that had been a single, junior officer's responsibility.

When the Torpedo Station was established, its staff consisted of Lieutenant Commander Matthews and six officers. Rotating rosters of approximately 20 officers in training were generated for those being instructed in mine warfare.

On October 12, 1869, the Bureau of Ordnance (BuOrd) authorized the employment of Professor Walter N. Hill, an acclaimed expert in pyrotechnology. Hill was the first of a series of highly qualified civilian chemists employed. As the Station became busier, additional civilians were hired. By the end of 1870, the Station's workforce numbered 24 employees.

By 1872, the Station's physical plant was in place and operational, with 21 Navy officers under instruction: six lieutenant commanders, 12 lieutenants, one master and two ensigns, and two civilian chemists, chief chemist Professor Hill, and assistant chemist T. M. Chatard. These men were working on various experimental underwater weapons, including towed, stationary, spar, and automobile torpedoes in addition to explosives and electrical devices.

Other personnel at NTS during the 1870s included Professor Moses G. Farmum, an "electrical expert," who worked at the Station for more than a decade. Another employee, H. A. Hardy, a so-called "constructor" devoted three years to overseeing the fabrication of the U.S. Navy's first "Fish" torpedo.

In the Station's early days, the management structure, with the exception of the chemistry and electrical professors, was military. Civilian support fell into two categories: the artisans such as machinists, metalworkers, electrical engineers and a Master Mechanic who acted as supervisor, a Chief Clerk, who answered to the Commanding Officer, and a civilian paymaster, who handled all finances. The Chief Clerk was in charge of all administrative matters and the Master Mechanic had the final authority in all artisan matters. As the machine shop became fully operational additional artisans were hired, and by 1880, the number of civilian employees had grown to 34.

Through the mid-1880s, Admiral Porter handpicked the Station's Commanding Officers, most having served with Porter during the Civil War, and the Station was sometimes referred to as "Porter's Torpedo Corps." An impressive number of these early officers eventually achieved flag rank, including Admiral Dewey, the hero of Manila Bay; Admiral William T. Sampson, who defeated the Spanish fleet at Havana; and Admiral Frank Friday Fletcher, who received the Congressional Medal of Honor for commanding naval forces at Vera Cruz in 1914.

Education and Training

In addition to training in the theory and application of these new concepts, Admiral Porter also wanted the new Torpedo Station to examine concepts for defensive systems to protect the fleet from attacks by these new weapons.

Education was a fundamental part of the Naval Torpedo Station's mission, and the first class of student officers came aboard shortly after the Station's founding in 1869. For the first three years, the classes were informal due to the lack of suitable training facilities. However, even during this early period, the staff prepared and presented to the student officers comprehensive lectures on the new torpedo technologies and their application in naval warfare. In addition, each class studied specific topics; for example, the class of 1869 addressed spar torpedoes, and each student officer had to write a comprehensive paper on the assigned topic and its application.

In February 1870, the Torpedo Station established a library in support of the ongoing educational and experimental programs. By 1894, the number of specialized books and texts relating to the unique work done at the station totaled 3,754 volumes.

In 1910, torpedo instruction separated from the gunnery school, and, in the period before the First World War, the station was providing instruction in such diverse fields as deep-sea diving, electricity, and printing.

Before and during the First World War, the Torpedo Station developed and manufactured torpedoes with specific delivery methods, including a towed torpedo and an aerial torpedo, as well as naval defense mines, harbor defense nets, and the training of sailors in the handling and deployment of both offensive and defensive weapons.

A Unique Salute for Distinguished Visitors

During the summer of 1875, Secretary of the Navy George M. Robeson (1869–1877), accompanied by a distinguished entourage including Admirals Porter and Rogers, Generals Burnside and Warren, Senator Cragin, Commodores Jeffers and Davis, Captain Jones of the British Royal Navy, and Professors Rogers and Cook paid an official visit to the Torpedo Station. The purpose was to witness experiments and demonstrations of conventional stationary torpedoes (mines) and the new self-propelled torpedoes under development.

In honor of the occasion, Station Commander K. R. Breese, decided to forego the traditional 19-gun salute and welcomed the Secretary of the Navy with a 19-torpedo salute. Professor Moses G. Farmer, the station's resident electrical expert set up 19 electrically activated bottom-mounted torpedoes in the shallow water between Goat Island and Newport and wired them to a control station on Goat Island. When the distinguished visitors arrived, they duly received a 19-torpedo salute as Professor Farmer used his *Farmer's dynamo-electric machine* to sequentially fire the torpedoes, sending a 50-foot column of water into the air as each torpedo exploded. It was a spectacular start for the demonstrations and the world's only recorded 19-torpedo salute.

During their two-day inspection, the visitors witnessed an extensive series of demonstrations and experiments to familiarize them with the work, including moored torpedoes, spar torpedoes, and the wire-guided self-propelled Lay torpedo. Mock battles were conducted during which Admiral Porter personally took over the helm of the torpedo boat *Alarm*. On the second day, demonstrations were held in the open waters west of Goat Island. For the grand finale, the station chemist, Walter Hill, provided a spectacular demonstration of the new Swedish explosive dynamite and nitroglycerin that he was making at the Station. A raft packed with 60 pounds of dynamite exploded, blowing the raft into splinters and sending a water column 100 feet into the air. Next, a mine with 100 pounds of nitroglycerin moored in 30 feet of water was set off; the concussion was felt two miles away in downtown Newport. Finally, an old hulk loaded with almost 500 pounds of dynamite was blown to pieces.

Building the Torpedo Station

The first order of business was to design the structural facilities. The Navy's initial presence consisted of a former army barracks, a few temporary buildings used as Academy classrooms during the Civil War, and three civilian employees. The building material from the demolished temporary classroom buildings and the materials salvaged from other smaller buildings was recycled for the station's first structure, a new storehouse.

The northern end of Goat Island, near old Fort Wolcott, was selected for the administrative offices, shop areas, and piers, all located on the east side of the island facing Newport. The chemistry laboratory and explosives' facilities were located on the west side behind Fort Wolcott's massive embankments facing Narragansett Bay to protect the other structures from damage if explosions should occur. The south end of the island acted as a residential area where the senior staff lived.

During the first five years the station grew rapidly as the buildings erected were the most critical ones to the operation. These were the machine shop, storehouses, electric and chemical laboratories, cottages for officers, the inspector's house, and offices built over the old barracks.

Explosives, Electricity, Equipment and Training

During the first three decades of its existence, the Naval Torpedo Station's expanding programs required new physical facilities to support them. So advanced were some torpedo experiments that actual experimental torpedoes were being artisan-made before the new buildings were ready for occupancy.

The first actual "torpedoes" manufactured, in 1870, on Goat Island were of the static submarine mine-type that had none of the self-propulsion machinery of later models. The amount of torpedo hardware produced was rapidly increasing. During the 1870s, the Torpedo Station's physical plant continued to expand. The electrical laboratory, the dispensary and apothecary followed the Station's first large permanent structure, the machine shop, and the existing chemistry laboratory and storehouse expanded. Newspaper reports from 1874 give accounts of experiments with mines detonated by electricity.

The physical plant of the facility was expanding with addition of new cottages built as officers' quarters. During the 1880s, quarters for the Seaman Gunners School and a powerhouse were constructed.

Commanders in Chiefs' Visits

By the end of the nineteenth century, Newport's reputation as a summer playground for the very wealthy was well established. Presidential visits to Newport were eagerly anticipated events. On July 5, 1889, President Benjamin Harrison arrived in Newport Harbor aboard the U.S. Navy steam cutter the *Dispatch*; he toured the Station and was briefed on the latest developments in torpedo technology. President Theodore Roosevelt was a frequent Newport visitor. He was a former Secretary of the Navy and as President was a constant advocate of a strong navy.

Electricity

As early as 1881, the inspection of a new system of electric lighting for Navy ships by a Board of Examiners judged the system "highly satisfactory." In 1887, the machine shop received wiring in conformity with a plan for wiring ships. When the demand for electricity aboard Navy ships increased, an experimental 200-watt dynamo was installed and the machine shop was wired to use the electricity generated. A new electrical laboratory permitted experiments with other equipment of interest to the Navy, such as motors, batteries, and firing devices. Extensive electrical experiments at the Torpedo Station stopped in 1909.

Primers

The primer factory, built in 1890, began manufacturing primers in 1891. An invention of considerable importance was the combination primer, which, as the name indicates, unites in one primer the forces of two different elements so that if the electricity should fail to act, the charge could still be fired by friction—which the primer also possessed. During the First World War the Station employed 800 workers to make primers, but this operation was discontinued in 1920.

Harbor Defense

Around 1892, Station interest in mines and nets for harbor defense led to the conversion of the old spar torpedo into a defensive mine. Manufacture and assembly of naval defense mines continued until 1915. Experiments with harbor defense nets and net-cutting torpedoes began in 1908 and continued, intermittently, until 1941

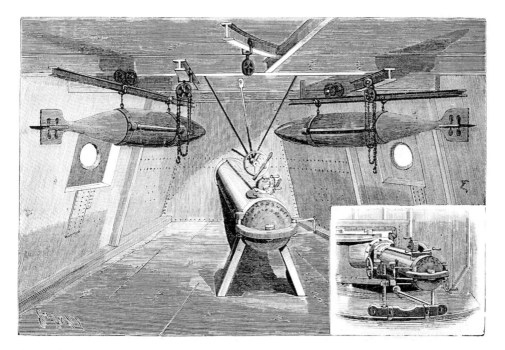

The Navy's first battleship, the U.S.S. *Indiana* (BB-1) was contracted in 1890 and launched in 1894; she was heavily armed and armored. She had four torpedo tubes capable of firing 18 inch Whitehead torpedoes. This image is a far-fetched idea of the *Indiana's* torpedo room by an illustrator unacquainted with warships' torpedo launching facilities.

Handling Equipment

By 1893, the Station was deeply involved in the manufacture of torpedo handling equipment, launchers, and guidance (fire control) devices; torpedo directors with guide bars and brackets. Handling equipment designed and fabricated at the station included trolley rails, switches, hoists, tail covers, and trucks for moving torpedoes around a ship's deck.

Gunners School

Officer and seaman training was a major function of the Station from its inception through to the First World War. A course of instruction for officers in the use of torpedoes in naval warfare began in 1873. Warrant gunners' training in the care, handling, and operation of torpedoes and explosives began in 1883. The Seaman Gunners School started in 1885. In 1910 a new curriculum was established. By 1921, 50 officers and 200 torpedo-men received training at the Station each year.

Printing Office

The Station's printing office was established around 1872. From its beginning, the printing office was of great value to the service. Operation and repair manuals were prepared containing descriptions of torpedoes, mines, compressors, appliances, and explosives manufactured and tested at the Station. These manuals served as an extension course to the service in the care, handling, and operation of projectiles and explosives. The printing operation transferred to Washington, DC in 1903.

For necessary repairs to ordnance buildings, magazines, gun parks, boats, lighters, wharves, machinery, and the like, $30,000 was authorized.

Guncotton

In 1881, the building of a large guncotton (nitro-cellulose) manufacturing factory began on the west shore, and for a number of years that explosive was made exclusively on Goat Island. Advances in the manufacture of guncotton led to an order from the Bureau of Ordnance, in 1882, for a daily production of 300 pounds for use in guns and torpedo charges.

Guncotton was the universally used explosive for torpedo warheads until about 1912. At that time, it was planned to use TNT (Trinitrotoluol) for all future warheads. The use of TNT started around 1911 and continued until the introduction of Torpex in 1930. Torpex was replaced by HBX in the 1940s, followed by H-6 in the 1960s. Torpex, HBX, and H-6, which were TNT with additives to increase the explosive yield, improve the stability, and reduced long-term storage deterioration. The explosive currently in use is PBX; this evolved in the early 1970s.

In 1895, fire destroyed the guncotton factory with some loss of life. It was thus determined impractical to mass in one building great quantities of that volatile explosive. Later, a number of small buildings were built into the embankment of the west shore. This scheme proved necessary with the introduction of smokeless powder. In each small building, a single step in the transformation of the raw cotton took place, thus reducing the danger of explosion.

The Navy acquired nearby Rose Island and built a large explosives magazine, a pier and a guard's cottage. Later, these remote facilities were used to load and store torpedo warheads.

Gould Island

In 1919, the Navy acquired Gould Island, another small island in lower Narragansett Bay, for the storage of torpedoes, warheads, and explosives. In 1921, two seaplanes at Gould Island became platforms for testing aerial torpedoes; they operated from a special taxiing ramp on the south end of the island. A large torpedo test launching facility occupied one-quarter of the island. Major construction included an overhaul shop and a firing range building jutting into the Bay like a giant breakwater.

By the turn of the century, the station was no longer the exclusive manufacturer of guncotton and smokeless powder. There was, however, continued production of primers and fuses, exploders and detonators, which fired guns and torpedoes. These were small round brass receptacles, one or two inches in length, filled in the case of primers and fuses, which ignite very fine gunpowder. However, the contents of exploders and detonators, which explode the guncotton in the torpedo and are more powerful, are composed mainly of fulminate of mercury.

Congressional Funding Restrictions

Beginning in the mid-1870s the U.S. Navy made annual requests to Congress for funding to purchase automobile torpedoes. Not until 1883 did Congress finally respond favorably to the Navy's request. However, Congress would only authorize payment after there had been conduction trials and a naval board had selected a specific design. The cost of the trials and the experimental vehicles were to be the responsibility of the interested vendors. Robert Whitehead and Louis Schwartzkopff, the leading European torpedo builders, refused to underwrite the cost of bringing their torpedoes to the United States for evaluation. They offered to demonstrate their wares in Europe, but the U.S. Navy was unyielding. On this basis, only three bidders qualified: the American Torpedo Company; an independent designer, Asa Weekes; and Commander J. A. Howell. Both the American Torpedo Company and Asa Weekes proposed surface-running rocket-powered torpedoes. Commander Howell proposed his flywheel-powered torpedo. In 1884, the Navy rejected the two surface-running torpedoes, but recommended further consideration of the Howell.

EXPERIMENTS WITH DETONATING GUN COTTON AT THE U. S. TORPEDO STATION, NEWPORT, R. I.—VIEW OF THE STATION.—[See p. 230.]

Illustrations of experiments with detonating guncotton at the U.S. Torpedo Station as described in the essay by Commander T. F. Jewell, U.S.N.

Spar, Stationary and Towed Torpedoes

Torpedo development in the United States during the nineteenth century experimented with many schemes. In May 1869, experiments started with a towed torpedo similar to the Royal Navy's Harvey torpedo. The Harvey consisted of two explosive-filled copper cases that followed some 150 yards behind the ship at a 45-degree angle, resembling modern minesweeping paravanes. The towed torpedoes exploded electrically by contact fuses. The Harvey torpedo, frequently referred to as an "Otter", swam at a diverse angle on a course roughly parallel to the towing vessel. Although obsolete by the mid-1870s, the Harvey torpedo remained in the Royal Navy arsenal well into the First World War.

One of the first pieces of experimental hardware built and tested at the Torpedo Station was a towed torpedo designed by Commanding Officer Matthews. This was made from 2-inch pine planks, 17 feet long, and 13.5 inches wide by 20 inches deep and initial tests were conducted in January 1870. The device consisted of a charge in a case with a fixed rudder towed off the ship's stern or beam. When underway the towline assumed an angle of about 45 degrees to the ship's centerline. When the torpedo contacted an enemy ship, the charge detonated electrically or by impact.

Experiments with spar torpedoes and mines continued, and by the 1870s, the Station was developing and testing new weapons. Although the U.S. Navy's first automobile torpedo was designed, built and tested at the Station during the 1870s, most of the early activity involved more conventional weapons such as spar torpedoes, towed torpedoes, explosives and the electrical devices used to fire them.

The 1870s saw an unusual number of inventive ideas from many sources. Officers at the Station expressed their creative talents by designing and evaluating an array of towed torpedoes. Endeavoring to improve upon the early designs of Commander Matthews, other developments by Lieutenants Barber, Maynard, and Converse, and even a design by Admiral Porter himself, were evaluated. Station work also concentrated on improving spar torpedoes. In 1876, the Torpedo Station purchased a steam-powered yacht from the Herreshoff Manufacturing Co., of Bristol, Rhode Island, for such spar torpedo experiments. The 55-foot steam launch, the *Lightning* costing $5,200 had a speed of 24 knots. Another Herreshoff steam launch, the *Spray*, joined the growing Station fleet in May 1879. Tests were conducted with these two launches against hulks employing spar torpedoes and towed torpedoes, evaluating the explosive charges and exploder devices.

In 1873, Captain Edward Simpson succeeded Commander Matthews as head of the Torpedo Station. Prior to taking command, Captain Simpson, on a mission in Europe, acquired a number of Harvey towing torpedoes from the British. Some of these were installed on U.S. Navy ships in the European squadron and the rest were sent to Newport for evaluation. Under Simpson's command, the Station discontinued developing an automobile torpedo, and emphasis shifted to towed and spar torpedoes.

By the mid-1870s, the Harvey towed torpedo had begun service on a U.S. Navy ship. Until 1880, the Torpedo Station was responsible for fleet issue of spar and towed torpedoes; this remained a major Station task until towed torpedoes were no longer used on American warships.

The June 15, 1877 issue of *Harper's Weekly* published this full page illustrating five methods of torpedo warfare. From the top, down: the radical steam propelled torpedo boat the *Alarm*; an outrigger steam propelled spar torpedo boat is attacking an iron clad war ship; a steam launch is laying down submarine mines to protect a harbor from an enemy's sneak attack; a Navy launch is laying electrical "counter-mines"; Whitehead's fish torpedo.

The speedy Herreshoff-built spar torpedo boat the *Lightning* is seen floating at ease near the east shore of Goat Island. In the background are officers' quarters, and the remains of old Fort Walcott's earthworks. In the upper left of this photo is the masonry archway, which Grace Herreshoff mentions in her monograph.

These photos originally appeared in the April 20, 1897 issue of the British military journal *The Navy and Army Illustrated*.

In the top photograph the steam launch is fitted with an outrigger spar torpedo prepared for attacking a mock-enemy vessel. When it is about to attack, the spar is run out over the bow until the head reaches a fork-shaped support. The explosive charge is dropped about 10-feet underwater and 22-feet horizontal from the launch's bow. For the safety of the crew, there is a steel shield just before the funnel where the crew controls the torpedo and maneuvers the vessel.

The bottom photograph attests to the powerful explosion obtained with a guncotton spar torpedo from a steam launch. The torpedo consisting of a charge of 35-pounds of guncotton has exploded against the hull of the "enemy".

Before ship deployment overseas, the Station staff was responsible for providing the torpedo suite, training the crew in its operation, inspecting the ship, and certifying that the torpedo suite was operational. Station staff was also responsible for ensuring that the "torpedo box" was included containing spare parts, tools, and detailed instructions about the torpedoes.

At Goat Island, the Navy experimented with high-speed steam launches for spar torpedo delivery. The contribution of Admiral David Dixon Porter was his invention of an iron steamer, the *Alarm*, armed with one heavy gun in the bow, a ram and torpedo spars projecting through the side several feet under water.

Defending against such iron craft as the *Alarm*, necessitated a larger and faster torpedo boat catcher—the destroyer. The design of such a vessel came from the genius of John Ericsson, a double hulled iron vessel that he named *Destroyer*. Besides her speed, the chief merit in the *Destroyer* was her armament consisting of a gun protruding from her bow, submerged several feet below her waterline. This gun discharged a shell or torpedo containing 250 pounds of explosives at a range of 250 yards from her target. Ericsson succeeded in demonstrating the effectiveness of his underwater gun.

5

Initial Rejection of the Whitehead Torpedo

The idea of using a self-propelled vehicle to carry the charge to a distant enemy was first successfully implemented by the Englishman Robert Whitehead, who managed an iron works in Fiume, (today called Rijeka), an Austro-Hungarian port city at the head of the Adriatic Sea. In 1866, he produced the first working, "automobile torpedo," powered by compressed air and capable of carrying an 18-pound dynamite charge for 700 yards at six knots. Just before the turn of the century, an Austrian, M. Ludwig Obry, adapted the gyroscope to the torpedo for directional control, and in a series of improved versions, the Whitehead Torpedo became the prototype automobile torpedo. It was quickly adapted by navies worldwide for use on small, swift and stealthy torpedo boats intended for attacking capital ships.

The first Whitehead Torpedo looked very different from those of today. It was built of steel, 14 inches in diameter, 16 inches at the fins, and weighed 300 pounds. Its explosive charge was 18 pounds of dynamite. The motive power was compressed air charged to a pressure of about 700 pounds to the square inch; and the air chamber was made of ordinary boilerplate. The speed of the torpedo, when running under favorable circumstances, was six knots over short distances.

The torpedo, although a marvel of ingenuity, was exceedingly erratic in its performances. In one important particular, it continually failed, and that was in the regularity with which it kept its proper depth in the water. At times, it would run skimming along the surface, while at others; it dived down to the depths and explored the bottom.

Lieutenant W. S. Hughes, U.S. Navy, made the following observations concerning the Whitehead Torpedo in his 1887 *Scribner's Magazine* article "Modern Aggressive Torpedoes."

The torpedo that has been adopted by nearly every naval power of Europe is known as the Whitehead, and belongs to what may be designated as the "projectile class," that is, having been started on its course toward the enemy; the operator retains no control of it. Most of the various types of this class are wholly submerged when operated against an enemy, and are generally arranged to run at a given depth below the surface, varying from five to 15 feet.

Naturally, one of the main objects of inventors of torpedoes, as well as of those engaged in other fields of invention, is financial profit. The Whitehead is the only torpedo that has

Top: A Whitehead Mk 3 torpedo developed at the Naval Torpedo Station—this photograph is from about 1894. *Bottom:* The innovative propulsion and rudder system of the Howell Automobile Torpedo, *c.* 1898.

yet proved a success in this respect. It is built of thin sheets of steel, is cigar-shaped, and is made in three sizes, the largest being 19 feet long by 16 inches diameter, and the smallest 9 feet by 11 inches diameter. The motive power is compressed air, carried at a pressure of about 70 atmospheres, in a cylindrical reservoir within the torpedo. The speed is about 25 miles per hour for a distance of 450 yards. The torpedo is divided into three sections containing, the charge of 70 to 93 pounds of guncotton; adjusting mechanism, wherein lies the secret of the inventor, and by which the hydrostatic pressure of the surrounding water is made to regulate the depth of immersion; and the air-engines and steering machinery. It is designed to be carried on board a very swift torpedo boat capable of overtaking the fastest ironclad, and, when within effective range, to be discharged from the boat with the steering rudder of the torpedo set in a position as to direct its course toward the enemy. The first motion, or "discharge," is effected through a guide-tube in the bow of the boat, either above or below the surface of the water, usually by means of a very small charge of powder, after which, upon reaching the water, the torpedo is propelled by its own engines. The explosion either may be made to take place either upon impact with the enemy or after the torpedo has run a given distance.

The following edited article by Captain Robert Hanna, U.S.A., titled "The Whitehead Torpedo in the United States" first appeared in an 1895 issue of *Harper's New Weekly Magazine.*

Three of the principal types of torpedoes known in modern warfare are the mine torpedo, the controllable torpedo, and the automobile torpedo.

The mine torpedo is located in some fixed position beneath the water, determined by the necessities of defense, so that when an enemy's vessel gets over it, it may be exploded by contact or by means of electric wires connected with the shore.

The controllable torpedo has a mechanism, which propels it through the water, and controls its direction by electric wires connected with the shore, so that it may be exploded by contact with an enemy's vessel.

The automobile torpedo, whose direction, speed, and depth are controlled automatically, has no such restricted uses as the two former, but may be fired from a vessel going at full speed, as well as at rest, and on the ocean, as well as in harbor.

The Whitehead automobile torpedo, often called the "fish torpedo," is the evolution of years of experiment, and has the distinction of success in actual war. It is the invention of an Englishman named Robert Whitehead, whose works are now at Fiume on the Adriatic, where he has for many years manufactured for most of the great naval powers of the world. The Whitehead and Schwartzkopff torpedoes are essentially the same, the latter being made in Germany, and in use in the German Navy. The sinking of the *Blanco Encalada* by a Whitehead Torpedo in the Chilean war, and the sinking of the *Aquidabã* by a Schwartzkopff torpedo in the late Brazilian war, is two instances of their recent use. In the war just concluded between Japan and China, our information, though meager, would indicate that torpedo boats and Whitehead Torpedoes have played a most important part.

All the great naval powers of the world seem to have admitted the importance and necessity of their use, and recent years have seen a constant interest in the various fleets of the world of a class of small vessels of great speed, called torpedo boats, carrying an armament of automobile torpedoes and rapid-fire guns.

In 1891, when General B. F. Tracy was Secretary of the Navy, the advanced condition of our Navy made it necessary, in order to keep up with other naval powers of the world, to supply ourselves with some reliable type of automobile torpedo. Such an initiative would at once place us on equality with the other naval powers of the world in this respect. At that time, although we had a torpedo boat, named the *Cushing*, under construction, almost completed, we had no automobile torpedoes.

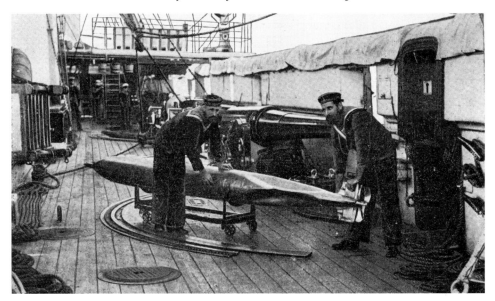

A Whitehead Fish torpedo is being inspected by British torpedo gunners aboard a pre-1900 wooden decked cruiser.

Sailors are hauling aboard what appears to be an E. W. Bliss manufactured Whitehead torpedo, developed in 1904.

The policy of the United States has always been opposed to buying war material abroad, and the question of supplying ourselves was a serious problem—that could be solved by having the Whitehead Torpedo made in this country.

Because of the Secretary's inquiries, Mr. E. W. Bliss, of Brooklyn, engaged to manufacture this torpedo, if the necessary arrangements could be made with the inventor abroad. To this end, a naval officer and a representative of the Bliss Company traveled to the Whitehead works at Fiume.

After the necessary arrangements were made, and some months spent in the study of the manufacture, they returned and the E. W. Bliss Company entered into a contract to manufacture and deliver one hundred eighteen-inch Whitehead Torpedoes of the latest type to the American Navy. Conditional that they are made fully as well in every respect as those manufactured abroad, and that they should be likewise adjusted for speed, direction, and depth.

The Whitehead Torpedo is nearly the shape of a porpoise; this mammal was the model used for its original design. Its building material is mainly sheet metal, weighing eight hundred fifty pounds, and is about twelve feet in length.

It is composed of four principal sections, the head, which carries the explosive, the flask, also known as the air-receiver, which is charged with compressed air at a pressure of 1,350 pounds per square inch. The escape of the air runs the engine and propels the torpedo. The immersion chamber just after the flask, in which is the apparatus for regulating the depth and position, being a pendulum and hydrostatic piston that control a movable, horizontal rudder at the tail of the torpedo, through a small air steering-engine connected with this rudder by a movable rod. This indispensable horizontal rudder corrects the depth of the torpedo. If the torpedo goes below its set depth, the rudder moves up, bringing the torpedo up and when inclined up or above its set depth, it reverses the operation.

The last section contains the engine, which is supplied with the compressed air from the flask by means of a pipe through a system of valves that regulate, automatically, the speed and duration of the run. The engine turns a shaft on which at the tail of the torpedo, are two propellers so geared to turn in opposite directions. On each side of the tail are the vertical rudders, which serve to control the direction. Their position is determined by experiment to cause the torpedo to run straight and is one of the most difficult of the adjustments.

There are two heads with every torpedo, which are interchangeable. The warhead is made of bronze and is charged with one hundred twenty pounds of wet guncotton. On the nose of this head is an apparatus called the pistol, which the motion of the torpedo through the water turns a small propeller at its forward end, which as it revolves frees a plunger, so that the impact at the target will force the plunger down upon a fulminate cap at its base and explode. This is in contrast with a tube of dry guncotton extending into a mass of wet guncotton, with which the warhead is filled. This dry guncotton possesses the property of exploding wet guncotton when coming in forcible contact with it. Therefore, when the torpedo is prepared for war, it is constructed so that no chance blow against it will cause it to explode; it must run a certain distance, sufficiently removed from the firing vessel before exploding, thus eliminate all possibility of damage.

The other head is made of thin steel [later of copper], and is ordinarily filled with fresh water, and the torpedo when equipped with this head may be fired an indefinite number of times. In service, it is used for practice. This torpedo is so constructed that when launched either from a gun above water or from a submerged frame beneath the surface, the engine is started in the act of launching, and it will run any distance required within a thousand yards. When it is used with the practice head, after completing its run, the engine stops automatically, the torpedo jumps out of the water and lies on the surface until picked up to be fired again.

When used with the warhead, it is adjusted to sink upon finishing its run, thus preventing its falling into the hands of the enemy in case of failing to strike the enemy vessel.

At the Whitehead factory on the landlocked bay of Fiume, where the weather, the tides, and the location were favorable, the problem of adjusting torpedoes presented many fewer difficulties than confront us Americans. There, it was practicable to charge the torpedoes with air in the factory, run them out on a dock at their doors, and launch them from a submerged frame, where they started at their set depth. This submerged launching eliminating one of the greatest difficulties in handling them. The attempt was at first made in New York Harbor to adopt the method of launching from a submerged frame by building a dock for this purpose. However, after long and expensive trials, engineers agreed the tides were so strong and so variable as to make all adjustments unreliable. The very object of the adjustment thus being defeated, as the torpedo, like a rifle bullet, must go where it is aimed, when not deflected by extraneous causes. When they are likely deflected, the naval officer, knowing the strength and direction of the currents, must make the necessary allowance in aiming the torpedo.

With the assistance of the Navy Department, a location was finally selected in the Peconic Bay, at the eastern end of Long Island, abandoning the expensive wharf in New York Harbor as a total loss. The decision by the Navy Department instructed that the torpedoes be adjusted by firing from a tube on the deck of a vessel in service. Therefore, it became necessary, to charter and finally to buy a steamer, which was, equipped with a torpedo tube, air pumps, and all the torpedo appliances of a regular torpedo boat.

Not until the summer of 1893, were the difficulties attending the adjustment of torpedoes under these conditions resolved. Now our Navy's cruisers receive their torpedoes adjusted for immediate use, and it is believed adjusted more nearly under the conditions of actual service than in any other navy in the world.

In this official 1894 U.S. Navy photograph an experimental Whitehead Mk 2 is being test-fired from the Naval Torpedo Station's east dock; in the background is torpedo boat TB-15, the *Talbot*.

Hawsers attached to four heavy anchors are placed at to hold the vessel stationary, mooring the vessel used as an adjusting station. A net two hundred felt long is anchored at the eight-hundred-yard range, so it hangs vertically in the water, the upper edge on the surface, the center marked by a flag. This is the target. At the net is a flat-bottom boat that is used as a station for the observer taking notes of the speed, depth, and deviation from the center, and is arranged to be moved to any point on the net.

The launching tube is sighted on the flag, and the torpedo having been charged with compressed air to a pressure of ninety atmospheres, of 1,350 PSI is inserted into the 'gun' through the breech, which is closed by an airtight door. The receiver on top of the gun is then charged, and the torpedo is launched by pressing a lever, which admits the air from the receiver in rear of the torpedo and forces it out. A small charge of black powder is sometimes used for launching the torpedo. It moves out almost noiselessly, the engine turning the propellers starting up automatically drives into the water with a splash and disappears. At this splash, the observer at the net starts his stopwatch and looks out for the torpedo, which can be followed by the air bubbles in its wake.

Endeavoring to get as nearly over the torpedo as possible, the observer stops his watch as it goes through the net. Because the torpedo is moving at about twenty-eight knots, and as the torpedo is in advance of the air bubbles, it requires a sharp eye and close observation to catch it. To the uninitiated, it looks like a flash of steel in the water. This speed in an object weighing eight hundred fifty pounds makes it a dangerous neighbor; even without the explosive, great care is necessary to avoid accidents. After passing the net, generally about one hundred yards, the engine stops automatically and the torpedo finishes its run, with a leap out of the water and floats until picked up by a launch which brings it back to the firing point with the record of its flight. It is recharged and fired again with such changes in adjustment as may be necessary until it is running as desired by the officer in charge of the experiments.

It must then be fired for acceptance, which is determined by the naval inspector present from the record it makes in five successive shots without change of adjustment.

It is required that the deviation from any set depth shall not exceed fifteen inches at a range of 800 yards, and that it may be set to run anywhere from five to twenty feet in depth, it will be seen that this torpedo may be depended upon to strike a vessel at almost any required point below the armor line, where the explosion upon impact will do the most damage.

The torpedo after passing the required running tests, are shipped to the United Sates Naval Torpedo Station at Newport, Rhode Island, where they are placed upon cruisers that are equipped with torpedo firing guns.

One hundred fifty torpedoes are presently stocked in the Torpedo Station's armory; the Secretary of the Navy authorized contracting for an additional fifty torpedoes.

Although costly, their actual value in war, when measured by possible results is imminence, when it is considered that one torpedo properly delivered will sink a man-of-war costing millions.

The moral effect is still greater. Nothing but a strong fleet would dare to approach our coasts if it were known that we were well equipped with torpedoes and torpedo boats as an adjunct to our Navy. The torpedo boats are generally painted such a color to be almost invisible at night; they are very low in the water, and almost noiseless when under way. In

The TB-14 *Morris* fires a Whitehead Mk 1 torpedo from her starboard tube while underway in Narragansett Bay about 1910.

A Torpedo Station Whitehead Mk 1 torpedo aboard the U.S.S. *Connecticut, c.* 1914.

recent experiments at Newport, when certain cruisers were warned that an attack would be made by the United States torpedo boat *Cushing* within half an hour; with all their search lights sweeping the horizon, and every one on deck was on alert, the *Cushing* repeatedly approached to within close torpedo range unobserved.

The commander of a torpedo boat in future wars must be prepared to risk everything in a rush at the enemy; for he will accomplish his objective if his torpedoes take effect, even if he loses his boat and all on board.

At present in our Navy, we have one torpedo boat, the *Cushing*. The *Ericsson*, just completed is awaiting acceptance. One of the possibilities of our future Navy is the introduction of a submarine torpedo boat armed with automobile torpedoes, which can attack the enemy in safety and unobserved.

Historic Retrospect

The following edited article by Robert G. Skerrett, titled "The Whitehead Torpedo" first appeared in the August 1904 issue of *The Technical World.*

The disastrously destructive work of passive submarine mines during the Civil War, crude though they were, set a number of inventive minds to thinking. In 1864, Captain Luppis of the Austrian Navy conceived a style of small fire ship, or "floating torpedo" which should be self-propulsive and dirigible [*sic*]. His idea was to propel the torpedo by clockwork, and to guide it to the target by lines leading back to a controlling base. After numerous experiments, he laid his scheme before the Austrian naval authorities, who rejected his proposed method to steer his torpedo. In the hour of his greatest difficulty, Captain Luppis turned over the problem of making something workable out of his own first crude notions to Mr. Whitehouse, a practical mechanic, then in charge of an engineering concern at the Austro-Hungarian port of Fiume, (today's Rijeka) on the Adriatic coast..

Whitehead promptly abandoned Captain Luppis' scheme, and proceeded to evolve a torpedo to run under the surface, which, when started on its destructive mission, should be self-controlled in every detail. After two years of work and experimentation, Whitehead's first torpedo was ready for trial. Having been built in secret, for only his son and a trusted fellow mechanic were let into the secret, its first appearance was even more startling.

Encouraged by the Austrian Government, who gave the torpedo extensive practical trials, Whitehead gradually evolved an improved order of the weapon, among other things, working out the primary idea of the "balance chamber," which now controls the torpedo's uniform depth of submergence. So precious was this secret deemed, that elaborate precautions were taken to keep the details from the world. A room with carefully shielded windows kept the curious from seeing in, while a sentry stood continually on guard at the door. Like most secrets, it eventually leaked, and the details of the mechanism proved to be beautifully and wonderfully simple.

From a weapon of most erratic performance, the torpedo has grown to be a marvelously precise instrument of war. Within its range, it is even more accurate than the best modern ordnance and less affected by local conditions. Today our own naval authorities are experimenting with an improved design—the result of purely American inventive genius—which promises to make the Whitehead in this new form even better and more formidable than before'.

Austria was the first government to show interest in Whitehead's invention. They conducted their own experiments with the new weapon during 1867–1869. As a result, Austria purchased the manufacturing rights from Whitehead, but permitted him to sell his torpedoes to other governments.

By 1895, Whitehead's torpedoes had been in use by most of the world's major naval powers for over a decade. Whitehead continually worked to improve the performance of his invention. In 1895, he added a gyro to his torpedo that controlled its course during the run to its target, thus converting the vehicle from a simple aimed projectile to a guided weapon.

Whitehead offered his torpedoes for sale to the navies of the world. In 1868, he offered two models: an 11-foot 7-inch model weighing 346 pounds with an explosive charge of 40 pounds of guncotton, and a 14-foot model weighing 650 pounds with an explosive charge of 60 pounds of guncotton.

Performance of the two models was about the same: 8-10 knots with a range of 200 yards. The offering price of these torpedoes was $600 for the smaller version and $1000 for the larger model.

The British Royal Navy became interested in the Whitehead Torpedo following a successful demonstration in 1869, and received their first delivery in 1870. In 1871, the Admiralty bought manufacturing rights, and production was started at the Royal Laboratories at Woolwich, London. With a short time, the British were manufacturing their own version of the Whitehead Torpedo, known as the 'Woolwich' or 'Royal Laboratory' pattern.

The French, German, Italian, Russian, and Chinese Navies followed the Royal Navy in purchasing the Whitehead Torpedo, and soon Whitehead was exporting his torpedo around the world. By 1877, the Whitehead Torpedo was attaining speeds of 18 mph for ranges of 830 yards or 22 mph for 200 yards. Air flask pressure also had been increased to approximately 1,100 psi.

By 1880, nearly 1,500 Whitehead Torpedoes had been sold to the following countries: United Kingdom, 254; Germany, 203; France, 218; Austria, 100; Italy, 70; Russia, 250; Argentina, 40; Belgium, 40; Denmark, 83; Greece, 70; Portugal, 50; Chile, 26; Norway, 26; and Sweden, 26.

Whitehead had achieved instant success with a novel weapon. The first experimental torpedo worked well and was being mass-produced for export within four years—an enviable achievement for any new product development.

Dissecting Whitehead's Torpedo—the Specifications

But how did Whitehead's devilishly clever invention actually work? The 18-inch Whitehead had a speed of 28.5 knots for a distance of 800 yards, it carried an explosive charge of 132 pounds of guncotton, its weight was around 1,200 pounds; air was stowed in a chamber to a pressure of 1,500 pounds to the square inch. This mechanical fish, which was 17 feet long, was made of the finest steel, and propelled from its "gun" or launching tube by a small charge of gunpowder or a blast of compressed air.

The Head

The torpedo contained two heads—the practice head and the warhead. The former was filled with water, while the latter contained a powerful charge of guncotton. Without some form of protection against accidental discharge, a torpedo became dangerous the moment its warhead and primer were in place. In order to prevent the striking rod from hitting the explosive primer of fulminate of mercury, there were two safety devices. First, if the torpedo was launched from a deck mounted firing tube, the first safety device was a small propeller threaded on the striking rod that held the rod firm until, through the action of the water as the torpedo ran its course for about fourteen yards, the propeller unscrewed itself, freeing the striking rod. Second, when the torpedo was in a submerged tube, if the vessel was underway, the wash of the water might work this safety propeller loose. As an added precaution, a strong copper shearing pin held the rod in place until the heavy blow of actual contact against the target broke the pin and drove the plunger against the primer.

For target practice, a nose, which could be hammered and banged without risk of detonation, replaced the warhead, ordinarily stowed securely in a special magazine, an innovative design if the practice head was made of copper soft enough to collapse on contact with a ship's side. The object was to score many actual hits safely, without loss of the torpedo or the practice target.

The explosive charge of 132 pounds of wet guncotton was insensitive to ordinary shock and could be roughly handled safely. To detonate the guncotton a very violent blow was necessary. This was the mission of the primer of six ounces of sensitive dry guncotton, and the initial detonating primer of some thirty grains of fulminate of mercury. When ignited, this expands to 2,500 times its normal size, and deals the dry guncotton a blow powerful enough to detonate the otherwise insensitive guncotton.

The Air Chamber

Immediately aft of the warhead was the air chamber, which, carrying air at a pressure of 1,500 psi had to be able to withstand a test pressure of 2,250 pounds. While the 18-inch Whitehead Torpedo carried air enough to propel the weapon for 2,000 yards, the torpedo, because of errors which multiplied with distance, had a limited range of 800 yards.

The Balance Chamber

Above the air chamber was the balance chamber, Whitehead's so-called "secret compartment." In this watertight space was the depth-controlling mechanism. The torpedo's balance mechanism consisted, primarily, of two parts—a delicately pivoted pendulum or weight, and a valve affected by hydrostatic pressure. The pendulum was connected with a controlling rod leading directly to the horizontal rudders at the torpedo's tail, which, moving up and down, controlled the weapon in a vertical direction. If the torpedo plunged by the head, the pendulum, moving longitudinally, swung forward and brought the horizontal rudder up, forcing the torpedo toward the surface until the weapon lay horizontal once more. A thick rubber diaphragm shielded the valve, connected to one of the pendulum's arms, from the water. The valve, activated by a coiled spring, was set to work at depths of 6 to 15 feet. If the torpedo started diving below its desired depth, the external water pressure, pushing against the rubber diaphragm and the spring, caused the valve rod to move just to the extent to which the water pressure overbalanced the set spring. This motion, in turn, transmitted to the horizontal rudders. The torpedo in this way was returned to its desired depth, where the spring again balanced the external water pressure, and the rudders returned to their normal position. Neither the spring nor the pendulum was powerful enough to work the rudders directly against the pressure of the passing water when at full speed. To aid them, a small servomotor controlled by the pendulum and the hydrostatic valve had ample power to move the rudders.

The Starting Valve

This valve turned the air on to the engines. It was actuated by a small lever projecting beyond the upper surface of the torpedo, which is tripped—thereby opening the air duct—as the torpedo left the tube. If the air was turned on full, the engines raced at 2,000 revolutions a minute, which could crack the torpedo's envelope. To prevent this, a small flat tripping lever controlled a delay-action valve that checked the passage of air until this tripping lever was thrown back by the water as the torpedo plunged and the propellers were submerged. Even now, the full pressure of air in the flask was not allowed to reach the engines. If it did—apart from the tax upon the engines—they would be driven at constantly reduced speed and the velocity of the torpedo would be uncertain. To prevent this, an ingenious reducing valve intervened between the air supply and the engines.

The Engines

The engines were of the compact three-cylinder Brotherhood-type. While the cylinders were less than 4 inches diameter, and the pistons had a stroke of but 3 inches, they developed energy equal to 56 hp. These engines drove directly on a single shaft, which, in turn, drove one of the two propellers. The other screw drove in the opposite direction. This is because the propellers were "rights" and "lefts," so that the resultant thrust was uniform and the torpedo launched directly ahead.

The Buoyancy Chamber

Above the engine compartment was the buoyancy chamber, which gave the torpedo the necessary levity. This buoyancy, when the air flask was charged at 1,350 pounds, was just zero. An interior steel girdle, withstanding outside pressure, securely braced this chamber. Also in this compartment was the gyroscope mechanism used for controlling the vertical rudders for horizontal steering.

The Gyroscope

Until the gyroscope, otherwise known as the Obry gear, appeared, the lateral course of the torpedo was very erratic. Any irregularities, such as dents in the torpedo shell, would cause it to steer badly. The gyroscope reduced the torpedo's undesired pitch and roll errors to a minimum.

The gyroscope was a finely balanced bronze top, weighting less than two pounds, very delicately hung like a ship's compass. This top was set spinning by a powerful spring, set free by the same lever that turned on the air as the torpedo left the tube; a velocity of 2,200 revolutions a minute was typical. The axis of the gyroscope wheel was aligned with the longitudinal axis of the torpedo. No matter how far the torpedo swung to right or left, the gyroscope remained in its original position: the direction where the torpedo was first aimed.

A Few Conclusions

Robert Whitehead was a mechanical genius. Through tenacious experimental efforts, he designed and developed a sophisticated self-propelled undersea missile with a "secret" dynamic depth control system. When dynamic control system theory finally reached scientific maturity in the 1950s, engineers learned that Whitehead's artisan experimental depth control was at best only marginally stable. His automobile torpedo had a major impact on naval warfare and strongly influenced the evolution of the Naval Torpedo Station.

U.S. Navy's Initial Rejection of Whitehead's Torpedo

In spite of the spectacular achievement of Whitehead's torpedo, two offers to sell the rights to the U.S. Navy, first in 1869 for $75,000, and again in 1873 for $40,000 were rejected.

According to E. William Jolie's *A Brief History of U.S. Navy Torpedo Development*, (1978) an industrial spy working for the Woolwich Laboratory was willing to turn over plans and specifications for the torpedo in return for employment at the Naval Torpedo Station.

Although the record indicates that the Navy declined the *sub-rosa* offer, a set of plans was obtained and turned over to Commodore Jeffers, then Chief of the BuOrd. The plans were not exploited, but were the subject of a lengthy exchange and quite probably legal proceedings between Commodore Jeffers and Robert Lines, Whitehead's U.S. agent, as reported in the press in the spring of 1881.

The Whitehead Torpedo, despite its wonderful potential, seems not to have impressed U.S. Navy tacticians. A paper on "movable torpedoes" published in 1873 states:

> Our conclusion is that the Whitehead-Luppis Torpedo is not adaptable to the combat of vessels on the high seas, but that it can be advantageously employed in the defense of ports and the attack of vessels surprised at anchor.

The Navy consensus was that the Whitehead Torpedo was too delicate, too complex, and too "secret".

The Whitehead Torpedo critics wrote of other defects in an 1889 publication:

1   Small explosive charge. Inefficiency due to the small charge carried, which is insufficient to destroy the hulls of vessels like modern ironclads that are divided into numerous watertight compartments.
2   Uncertainty as to accuracy. For, although a vessel can generally be hit up to a range of 3000 yards, this cannot be depended upon, the course of a Whitehead occasionally being very erratic, especially with over-water discharge from the broadside of a vessel at speed. Moreover, during handling and discharge, the fins, and rudders, and other gear projecting from the body of the torpedo are liable to derangement, due to imperfections in the design or manufacture of the automatic controlling gear.
3   Expense. The manufacturing cost of one Whitehead being over £500, to which is added the share of price first paid for the patent, and the cost of the discharging appliances.
4   Intricacy. The torpedo contains a quantity of highly finished and complicated machinery.
5   Maintenance. Constant attention and care is required to keep the torpedoes and their impulse arrangements clean and efficient.
6   Manipulation. Great intelligence on the part of personnel combined with a long and careful training, being essential.
7   Loss of control after discharge. When combined with the uncertainty as to accuracy already mentioned, increases the difficulties attending the employment of these torpedoes in fleet actions.
8   Motive power danger. The highly compressed air does sometimes burst the torpedo. Hostile shot would increase this danger.
9   Space occupied. Especially when those of the appurtenances are taken into consideration.

In addition to these criticisms, the small swift torpedo boats specially built to carry the Whitehead Torpedo were regarded with little favor. They were deemed too small to carry a crew at sea for long voyages. It also turned out that all boats designed as Whitehead Torpedo firing platforms were too large and cumbersome to be hoisted onboard a man-of-war, and yet too small to be sea-going themselves; they were relegated to harbor or river defense.

It is unsurprising that during this early period of automobile torpedo development (1870–1880) the U.S. Navy content itself with furthering the sophistication of the spar and towing torpedoes primarily through the addition of electrical detonation features.

Torpedo Station's Fish Torpedo

Torpedo development in the United States from 1870–1900 saw experiments with many schemes. Chemical, electrical, and rocket propulsion were all attempted, and surprisingly, guidance and power supply by a trailing wire was also popular. The guided wire torpedo became highly refined and employed on submarines during the mid-twentieth century. The Naval Torpedo Station was the site of many of these experiments.

Early torpedoes were fusiform or spindle shaped, with no straight cylindrical section between the nose and the tail. This shape was based on the theory that the long tapered nose would cut through the water more efficiently.

In 1883, a committee met in Britain to study various aspects of torpedo design. A respected hydrodynamicist, Dr. R. E. Froude, stated that the blunt nose of a torpedo offered no speed disadvantage, and would permit a larger explosive warhead.

The committee using a Whitehead Torpedo and a Royal Laboratories torpedo, each fitted with both pointed and blunt noses, conducted comparative tests. The tests showed that the blunt nose offered a full knot speed advantage over the pointed nose. This meant that more volume could be devoted to carrying explosives and air for propulsion without sacrificing speed. The ultimate in blunt nose design during this period appeared about 1909 with the American hemispherical heads.

After reviewing the report submitted by Lieutenant Commander Marvin who had visited Whitehead's factory, Admiral Porter sent an action memorandum to Commander Matthews asking him to "examine closely into the subject and ascertain if torpedoes of this plan cannot be gotten up." In turn, Matthews proposed that the Torpedo Station design and build an automobile-type torpedo similar to Whitehead's Fish. He went on to generate the following specification for the U.S. Navy's first self-propelled torpedo:

- To go underwater to a considerable distance at a fair rate of speed.
- To deviate neither to the right or left, and
- To proceed to and keep at a constant depth underwater no matter whether started on the surface or at any point beneath it.

With specifications approved during the winter of 1870, construction of the torpedo got underway in May. Matthews, with Lieutenant F. M. Barber and H.A. Hardy, then worked on the development and building of this weapon.

Although Marvin's report provided much detail about the external shape and construction of Whitehead's Torpedo and its performance in the water, no information was available on its internal components. Matthews and his assistants faced the formidable task of designing a complete, self-propelled torpedo from scratch.

The Station's torpedo body was to consist of three separate castings: (1) the front, warhead section, (2) the center, air flask section, and (3) the after body, containing the propulsion system. The plan was to solder inside the shell a copper tank containing carbonic acid, the gas from which would act as the motive agent. For the initial design, a static balance chamber was developed to control the vehicle's depth by adjusting the buoyancy to keep it at a preset depth as it ran through the water.

Because the Torpedo Station did not have any manufacturing facilities, Matthews had the various components fabricated by civilian contractors. The patterns and shells were made in Providence, Rhode Island; the depth bellows in Billerica, Massachusetts, and the rotary engine and propellers in Washington, DC. When the parts started to arrive, in the spring of 1870, Matthews encountered substandard hardware produced by the lowest bidder. The casings were full of flaws and the blowholes had to be "sweated full" before the shells could be machined. The Wheeler rotary engine, which from Barber's drawings looked like a reaction impulse turbine, leaked badly and failed to function properly. In addition, the gases from the carbonic acid generator caused severe corrosion. Attempts to repair the engine and reduce the leakage failed. Finally, in March 1871, Matthews proposed the design for a new engine to replace the troublesome one.

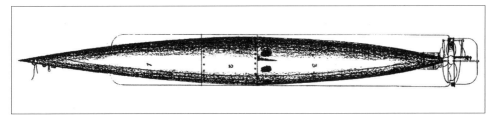

The top image is a graphic representation of Whitehead's 1866 Fish torpedo. Using information obtained after viewing Whitehead's invention at his Austrian laboratory in 1869, The U.S. Navy built its version (bottom photo) of the "fish" automobile torpedo at the Newport Naval Torpedo Station. Tests began in March 1871, using converted steam launches.

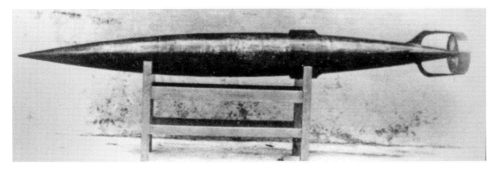

The new design was a two-cylinder horizontal cam engine called a "diamond" engine. The drive mechanism, which included a 3.5:1 gear reduction, was similar to that used for whip drills designed to drive the propeller at 250 rpm for 1,300 yards. The new engine checked out satisfactorily using steam, but the severe corrosion problems continued with use of carbonic acid gas. These corrosion problems led to a decision to use compressed air to power the Station's Fish torpedo. A special order for a high-pressure air compressor to charge the air flask delayed further testing.

While waiting for the new air compressor, Matthews decided that the static bellows idea he had designed to control the buoyancy of the torpedo would not work satisfactorily in a dynamic moving vehicle. He began a redesign of the depth control mechanism by changing his original idea of pumping seawater ballast to maintain a constant depth. Instead, he attached a set of balanced fins made active by the depth bellows. If the torpedo was deeper than the set depth, the bellows gave the fins an "up-elevator" signal, and if the torpedo was running shallow, the bellows transmitted a "down-elevator" signal to increase the torpedo's running depth. Since it was an undamped control system, the torpedo's depth trajectory tended to oscillate around the present depth giving it varies marginal depth control.

The first of six tests of the Station's Fish torpedo were conducted in June 1871. The first test ran without the new air compressor. With the carbonic acid gas generator in place, the torpedo immediately dove to the bottom and filled with water. Upon recovery, inspection discovered the engine clogged, the piston rods bent, and the engine badly corroded by the carbonic acid. Further tests were postponed until the arrival of the new air compressor.

The new compressor arrived in early July and by the end of the month the Fish torpedo was ready for its second in-water test. The torpedo disappeared beneath the water and ran for approximately 200 yards deviating only slightly to port. Although the torpedo was set to run at a 10-foot depth, the propeller occasionally broke the surface indicating a somewhat erratic depth performance. After the 200-yard run, the torpedo envelope again filled with water and sank to the bottom of Narragansett Bay.

Four design changes were made because of the failed third trial. (1) the size of the air tank was increased, (2) the size of the fins was increased, (3) the size of the vertical guards was reduced to save weight, and (4) a governor was installed on the engine.

In September three more launches of the Fish torpedo failed. The failures were not down to any design fault, but rather to extreme bad luck. The torpedo's first launch on September 11 at low tide became fouled in eelgrass near the wharf. Relaunched, it ran only 100 yards before tangling in eelgrass again. On September 26, a third trial launch was attempted; the torpedo became stuck in a mud bank, running until its fuel was exhausted. This failure was attributed to poor aim at launch.

To fix the aiming problem, Commander Matthews and Lieutenant Barber devised an aiming rod to attach to the air tube to aid in directing the torpedo to its intended target, but even with this addition, the torpedo strayed from its course. There were no further in-water tests of the Fish torpedo.

Matthews paid a visit to Whitehead at his Fiume factory on the Adriatic to view first-hand his latest torpedo improvements. Upon returning to Goat Island, he began designing a newer version of his Fish torpedo. He submitted his redesign, incorporating many of Whitehead's new concepts, to the Navy Department.

Matthews was transferred to a new command and his assistant Lieutenant Barber had a transfer due within a year. Consequently, the new torpedo design never reached hardware status. Although it never went into volume production, the design of a complex self-propelled, undersea weapon and its testing was a significant accomplishment.

Characteristics of the Naval Torpedo Station's Fish Torpedo

DIAMETER:	14 Inches
LENGTH:	12 Feet 6 Inches
WEIGHT:	420 to 430 Pounds
SHAPE:	Spindle with a 66-foot radius
WARHEAD:	70–90 Pounds of guncotton
PROPELLER:	Four-bladed, 1-foot dia.,
	4-foot pitch shroud over the propeller
ENGINE:	Wheeler rotary
EXHAUST:	Through the hollow propeller shaft
PROPELLANT:	Gas generated from Liquid carbonic acid

The Howell Torpedo

In 1871, Lieutenant Commander John A. Howell, U.S.N.[4] received a patent for his innovative flywheel-powered automobile torpedo. His patent also claimed that the flywheel could be used to control the torpedo's directional accuracy, but this claim was disallowed. Howell continued to tinker with his concept, and between 1871 and 1877, he built a series of small operational models that showed considerable promise. In 1877, a Naval Board gave Howell's torpedo design a favorable review and authorized the construction of a full-sized operational model. The first flywheel-powered torpedo design used a centrifugal pump as a propulsion-device by sucking in water and pumping it out the rear to provide thrust.

The Bureau of Ordnance contracted to have three Howell torpedoes made and shipped to Newport. The Bureau directed Torpedo Station Commanding Officer Commander William T. Sampson to conduct extensive evaluations of these new torpedoes. The first, tested on August 5, 1885, promptly sank to the bottom of Newport Harbor. On August 10, the second torpedo was launched and, after a brief run sank. Since the flywheel-powered torpedo was wakeless, it was almost impossible to determine the exact direction it was running in and extremely difficult to locate in the murky harbor waters. With two of the three units lost, the test program was put on hold while divers tried to locate the missing torpedoes.

After retrieving the lost units, The Bureau of Ordnance directed that a new testing site with clear water be found to observe the track of the torpedoes. The site selected was

Lake Michigan. By July 1886, the Howell prototypes were demonstrating consistently successful in-water runs, which led to the Howell being the first automobile torpedo issued to the American fleet.

In 1888, Howell sold his patent rights to the Hotchkiss Ordnance Company, makers of the famous Hotchkiss machine gun; they began production of Howell torpedoes in their plant on Fountain Street in Providence, Rhode Island. Hotchkiss built a test range in the Sakonnet River, in Tiverton, Rhode Island. An inspector from the Naval Torpedo Station witnessed the tests.

Hotchkiss produced several hundred Howell Mk 1 torpedoes. The torpedo's specifications for the time are impressive: 14.2 inches diameter, 11 feet long, 100-pound warhead, and a maintained speed of 25 knots at a 400-yard range with a maximum range or 700 yards. A 132-pound flywheel spun up to 10,000 rpm powered the torpedo. The brass torpedoes were superb examples of the high quality craftsmanship that American artisans produced in the late nineteenth century.

The Torpedo Station proudly displays its torpedo development progress with this float in a Newport Independence Day parade around 1910. The piggyback riders are a 12 inch Howell torpedo developed *c.* 1880, and 21 inch Whitehead Mk 5 developed *c.* 1901.

6

A Plethora of Inventions

With the rejection of the Whitehead torpedo, the Station was busily involved over many years testing other candidates and weapons ideas. As seen above, the winning design had been Lieutenant Commander Howell's patent, but some other ideas merited investigation.

The Zalinski Torpedo Gun

Polish born U.S. Army Lieutenant Edmund Louis Gray Zalinski, a recognized inventor and engineer, worked for two years (1885–1887), developing a novel and formidable weapon. In his official report to Secretary of War William Crowninshield Endicott, he described his invention as a "pneumatic, dynamite torpedo gun."

Lieutenant W. S. Hughes enlightens readers in his 1887 article with the following succinct description of Zalinski's new torpedo gun:

The barrel of this remarkable piece of ordnance is 60-feet long, made of iron tubing, and lined with brass to give a smooth interior. It throws a cylindrical brass or steel torpedo, eight inches in diameter, carrying a charge of 60 pounds of dynamite, a distance of 2¼ miles. Compressed air, as the name of the gun implies, is the projection force employed, the rear end of the gun-barrel is connected with an air reservoir kept under great pressure by an engine and any suitable pumping machinery. The gun is so accurately balanced on its supports, and the mechanical arrangements are so perfect, that but one man is required to aim and fire it. It is loaded at the breech, and the discharge is effected by a 'firing lever,' which opens the valve of the reservoir, allowing the highly compressed air to enter the gun behind the torpedo, and as the latter leaves the muzzle the valves close automatically. The charge is exploded by means of an electric fuse, the current for which is derived from a small battery carried within the torpedo. The forms of this fuse have been designed—one closing the circuit and causing the explosion upon impact with the enemy's vessel, by forcing back a small steel plunger projecting from the extreme forward end of the torpedo; while the other, requiring to be moistened in order to render the battery active, ignites the charge after the torpedo has sunk below the surface of the water.

During the Spanish-American War, Zalinski's pneumatic dynamite torpedo gun saw use on the U.S.S. *Vesuvius;* she mounted three 15-inch cast iron pneumatic guns, forward side-by-side at a fixed elevation of 16 degrees. The dynamite torpedoes were fired at Cuban shore batteries, rendering severe damage upon the enemy.[3]

The Lay Wire-Guided Torpedo (1872)

John L. Lay, of Buffalo, New York, one of the first American inventors to approach the U.S. Navy with his idea of a self-propelled torpedo, was talented, but his weapon designs were complex and very difficult to operate. In 1866, while installing mines (then referred to as torpedoes), controlled by a wire linked to a shore station, Lay came up with the idea of using electrical commands to steer torpedoes using a launch with a revolving reel of wire strung from the shore out to the weapon. Lay reasoned that if commands could be wired to the torpedo, it would be feasible to build an unmanned self-propelled weapon for harbor defense.

Lay's first model was a surface-running, semi-submersible boat-like torpedo, 30 inches in diameter, 25 feet long, and trimmed to run almost submerged. Powered by a carbonic acid gas driving a two-cylinder engine; Lay's wire-guided torpedo was controlled by a reel of wire connected to a firing station that transmitted steering commands to the torpedo during its run.

Lay's first model was a surface-running, semi-submersible boat-like torpedo, 30 inches in diameter, 25 feet long, and trimmed to run almost submerged. Powered by carbonic acid gas driving a two-cylinder engine controlled by a reel of wire connected to a shore-based firing station transmitting steering commands to the torpedo during its run.

The explosion is caused on contact if it is desired, or it may always be kept under the operator's control. Some of these boats [torpedoes] have but one wire in the cable, over which the various functions are caused to operate; others have a multiple cable, with a wire for each thing required to be done. Over a mile and a half of wire is carried so that the effective range becomes very much greater than that of any of its rivals.

Torpedoes and Torpedo Boats, 1882

Lay brought his torpedo to Egypt where he conducted a series of demonstrations. The Egyptian Government, impressed, purchased it in January 1871. Lay returned home and offered his torpedo to the U.S. Navy.

In 1872, the U.S. Navy prepared a contract specification for a Lay torpedo that started, stopped, steered, and ran a distance of two miles at a speed of 8 mph. The second Lay torpedo, developed in conjunction with the Torpedo Station and designated Lay Torpedo No.1, was larger, measuring 36 inches in diameter and 29 feet long, weighing some 4 tons, and carrying a 500-pound warhead ballasted to provide 200 to 300 pounds of buoyancy. It also included sight rods fastened at each end of the torpedo—flags or lights to assist in controlling its operation. The re-designed steering apparatus improved the vehicle's reliability. The Navy later rejected Lay's torpedo after discovering it did not reach contract speed. Lay worked to improve his weapon, and in October of 1875 introduced another model for testing. This model performed better than the previous version but still failed to meet the contract speed of 8 mph and rejected.

Lay sold later versions of his wire-guided torpedo to Russia, Peru, and Egypt. The Pratt & Whitney Company of Hartford, Connecticut manufactured most of the units.

The Controllable Auto-Mobile Torpedo

[An] American invention ... belongs to what is termed the "controllable class," that is, an operator stationed at some place of safety on shore sends it out alone to attack the enemy, guiding it in the desired direction by means of an electric cable which is coiled in a compartment of the torpedo and uncoils as the latter proceeds on its course. This torpedo is constructed of sheet-copper, is fusiform, or cigar-shaped, about 36 feet long by 22 inches in diameter, and is sustained at a depth of 3 feet below the surface of the water by a hollow copper float, to which it is attached by upright bronze rods. This float is itself somewhat longer than the torpedo, and may be repeatedly perforated by the enemy's bullets without destroying its buoyancy. The torpedo is propelled by its own engines, developing 45 horse-power, the motive power being carbonic acid gas, which, as is well known, becomes liquefied under a pressure of forty atmospheres. The liquid gas is carried in a small tank within the torpedo, and on its passage to the engines, through a coiled copper tube, is highly expanded by an intense heat produced by the chemical action of dilute sulfuric acid and quicklime. It has a speed of 20 miles per hour, which is greatest at the end of its run, and a range of 1 mile. The steering mechanism is controlled by an electric cable containing two copper wires; upon passing a current through the wires, one end of a balance lever is attracted, and the torpedo moves to the right; when the current is reversed the opposite end of the lever is attracted, causing the torpedo to turn to the left. The torpedo is divided into four separate compartments, the forward one carrying a charge of 200 pounds of guncotton or dynamite, and the others containing, respectively, the gas reservoir, the coiled cable, and the engines and steering machinery. At its extreme forward end, the torpedo is provided with a percussion-lock, which ignites the charge upon impact with the enemy's ship.

Lieutenant W. S. Hughes U.S.N.

The Sims-Edison Torpedo (1889)

The Sims-Edison torpedo is another type of the controllable class, and in its construction and general appearance very closely resembles that just described, but it differs from the latter in some important respects. The power by which the Sims-Edison is propelled, steered, and exploded is electricity. The requisite electric current is generated by a dynamo-machine on shore and conveyed to the torpedo by a flexible cable containing two wires, one of which supplies the motive power to the engine, while the other actuates the steering machinery. So complete is the control of the operator over this torpedo that he can easily cause it to maintain a perfectly straight course, turn to the right or left, moving a circle, or dive under obstructions. In order that the position of the torpedo may be always known to the operator, two hinged guide-rods, projecting upward from the float to a height of about two feet above the surface of the water, are surmounted by small globes, and at night carry differently colored lanterns, so screened as to be invisible from ahead. For convenience in handling, the torpedo is made in four sections, which can be quickly put together, and no one of which weighs more than 800 pounds. It has a speed of about 11 miles per hour, with a range limited only by the length of its cable, and carries a charge of 250 to 400 pounds of dynamite, which is exploded at the will of the operator by an electric fuse. A series of trials, under the supervision of Gen. Henry L. Abbot, Corps of Engineers, made at Willet's Point, New York, during the last six years [*c.* 1880], has resulted in the purchase of a number of these torpedoes by the United States Government.

Lieutenant W. S. Hughes, U.S.N.

The Lay-Haight Torpedo (1883)

In 1881 George E. Haight, supervisor of construction of the Lay torpedoes at Pratt & Whitney, built an improved model along the lines of Lay's invention. Haight's torpedo was 23 feet long with a 19-inch diameter that could obtain a speed of 12 miles per hour.

On January 15, 1881, the Bureau of Ordnance contracted Haight to produce one of the Lay-Haight torpedoes for evaluation. The Torpedo Station took delivery of the torpedo that summer, and conducted a series of trials. Although speeds exceeded more than 12 miles per hour, the torpedo did not survive the legal problems surrounding ownership and patent rights.

Ericsson's Projectile Torpedo (1873 and 1877)

John Ericsson had invented a torpedo powered by compressed air fed through a rubber hose from the shore. In 1873, Ericsson conducted private trials in Long Island Sound to evaluate his design. Satisfied that his idea was superior to Lay's, he asked the U.S. Navy to test and judge his new torpedo.

The Navy conducted a series of trials, but rejected the torpedo because its slow speed combined with an unreliable control system severely limited its potential. Undaunted, Ericsson started again, and in 1877 the Torpedo Station tested his improved model. The improvements did little to correct the basic problems, and the maximum speed only reached 4 miles per hour. Other problems plagued the test runs, so Ericsson ended his test program.

A tireless and prolific inventor, Ericsson was back at the Torpedo Station in the early 1880s with a new rocket-powered torpedo. Rocket propulsion, he believed, would provide a dramatic solution to the slow speed. Although Ericsson's rocket torpedo was fast, its trajectory was very unpredictable, making it a menace to everything in its firing range.

> The result of [Ericsson's] years of study and experimentation is the Destroyer, armed with a torpedo-gun which discharges under the water a projectile carrying a charge sufficient to sink the largest iron-clad afloat. The submarine gun is mounted in the bow of the vessel, near

A tireless inventor, John Ericsson conceived and built a torpedo powered by compressed air fed through a rubber hose and dispensed by the torpedo as it is traveling through the water. In this photograph, the boxy torpedo is awaiting tests at the Torpedo Station.

the keel, and is thus nearly ten feet below the surface of the water. It consists of a cylinder of gunmetal, or steel, 30 feet long, additionally strengthened at the breech by broad steel rings. It is loaded at the breech, the muzzle being incased by the vessel's stem, and closed by a valve to exclude the water. This valve is opened by suitable levers just before the gun is to be discharged and closes automatically as the projectile leaves the muzzle. The projectile is a steel torpedo, 25 feet long, 16 inches in diameter, and carrying a charge of 300 pounds of guncotton. It has a range of 300 feet during the first three seconds of its flight. The form of the torpedo is cylindrical, with a conical point in which is placed the percussion-lock and firing pin, and the explosion takes place upon impact.

Lieutenant W. S. Hughes, U.S.N.

In the 1890s, Ericsson returned yet again with another new invention; an underwater gun using compressed air to fire a projectile filled with dynamite or guncotton. The Navy bought a number of Ericsson's rocket guns and installed them on a few ships, including the U.S. Navy's submarine torpedo boat the *Holland.* However, concerns about the shock sensitivity of dynamite and the compressed air guns halted any practicable use of this new weapon.

Barber's Rocket Torpedo (1873)

Lieutenant F. M. Barber, U.S.N. who had participated in designing the Naval Torpedo Station's Fish Torpedo, designed his version of the rocket torpedo. The Torpedo Station built and tested one unit during the 1870s but discarded it due to its erratic performance.

The Schwartzkopff Torpedo Purchase

In 1873, L. Schwartzkopff, later known as Berliner Machinebau A.G. (Berlin Machine Building Co.), began manufacturing torpedoes based on the Whitehead design. Characteristics of the Schwartzkopff torpedo were: length, 14 feet 9 inches; diameter, 14 feet; speed, 22–25 knots for 220 yards, 22–23 knots for 440 yards; weight, 616 pounds; flask pressure, 1,500 psi; explosive, 44 pounds guncotton.

Schwartzkopff gained permission to sell his invention only to certain countries designated by the German government: Russia, Japan, and Spain. Because the Schwartzkopff torpedo was made entirely of bronze rather than steel as the Whitehead, corrosion resistance was one of the main selling points.

In 1898, the U.S. Navy purchased 12 Schwartzkopff torpedoes from a secret vendor. A European nation, possibly Austria, also purchased this weapon. However, comparable tests with the Whitehead Torpedo demonstrated its overall superiority over the Schwartzkopff version. The U.S. experience was probably the same since this was the only U.S. Navy purchase of a Schwartzkopff torpedo.

The Flying Devil

In 1893, in New Bedford, Massachusetts, shoemaker Robert Cunningham asked the Navy to evaluate his rocket torpedo. Like its predecessors, the Cunningham Rocket Torpedo had an erratic trajectory when fired that limited its usefulness. The Torpedo Station tested Cunningham's rocket torpedo for several years; test firings were from a submerged tube. Lack of accuracy and wide variations in speed were major problems that kept rocket torpedoes from leaving the experimental stage.

On July 4, 1897, Cunningham, filled with 100 proof spirits and patriotic enthusiasm, rolled his invention out of his yard and into the street. Straddling the torpedo, he planned to ride it at the head of his personal parade. While astride his rocket propelled torpedo, he attempted to set it off with a burning newspaper torch. His son disarmed him.

Not to be denied, Cunningham ignited his torpedo with matches and it blasted off. Fire shot from the portholes and the tail of the weapon. Hissing as it went; the torpedo scorched two horse drawn carriages in its wild flight. People and horses scattered, running from its path until, finally, it smashed into a tree stump and exploding violently setting fire to five houses and a butcher's shop. Luckily, the only human casualty was a startled bystander who lost half of his handlebar mustachio to a piece of flying metal! From that day on, townsfolk knew Cunningham as the "Wild Irishman," and his torpedo "The Flying Devil."

In 1898, Cunningham built more rocket torpedoes, and was again ready to demonstrate his wonderful invention. For his test firings, he bought the schooner *Freeman* and installed a torpedo tube, designed by him, in the forward part of her hold. It was a drawn steel tube, 20 feet long and 16 inches in diameter, weighing two tons. It projected about a foot through the hull of the *Freeman*, just beside the cutwater, and was parallel to the keel on the starboard side. Steel straps 5 inches wide and 1 inch thick were bolted to the timber bed to hold the tube in position. When the breech closed, it became watertight by pressure. A cable ran from a battery on deck, through a hatch, to the tube in the hold, supplying electrical current.

The first torpedo fired ran for forty feet before it buried itself deep in the muddy bottom of Buzzards Bay. The second torpedo exploded in the tube; tearing such a hole in the *Freeman's* hull, that she sank almost immediately.

This ill-fated venture marked the end of Cunningham's attempts to develop a rocket torpedo. However, the Navy did not abandon his idea of rocket technology; it was resurrected later to become one of our modern warships' weapons.

The Patrick Torpedo

The Patrick Torpedo was a dirigible-type vehicle with a 41-foot-long float. Testing commenced in the late 1880s. This wire-guided weapon electrically controlled through a cable 7,000 feet in length, attained speeds of more than 20 miles per hour during trials. The actual weapon, suspended from its float, was about three feet under water; it was 36

Robert Cunningham and his rocket torpedo. The Torpedo Station tested Cunningham's torpedo for several years; test firings were from a submerged tube. Lack of accuracy and wide variations in speed were major problems that kept rocket torpedoes from leaving the experimental stage.

feet long by 22 inches diameter, and carried an explosive charge of about 200 pounds of dynamite.

The Navy, impressed with the Patrick's performance, purchased three for testing at the Torpedo Station. In 1892, the Patrick was accepted for service use. The Patrick was primarily a defensive torpedo designed to protect fleet anchorages and harbors, so none entered the fleet.

The Hall Torpedo.

In the late 1890s, testing of the Hall began at the Torpedo Station. Invented by Lieutenant Hall, his design used a high-pressure, high-temperature flask of water heated to 550° F to generate steam to power the weapon. Since the steam contained more energy than the cold-compressed air used by the Whitehead Torpedo, the Hall had better performance.

The need to have a steam boiler fired and the time required to heat the water tank limited the torpedo's operational ability. However, Hall's innovative use of hot gases to increase torpedo performance set the stage for "hot gas" torpedoes that became

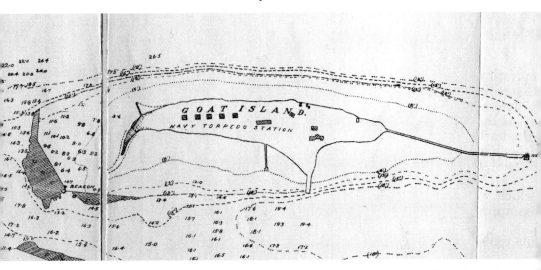

This map of diminutive Goat Island was drawn on July 31, 1884 by Lieutenant E. H. Elliot, Corp of Engineers. It was well known since colonial times that the island held a strategic defensive location in Newport Harbor.

the standard within a few years. The Naval Torpedo Station, at this time, also became involved in designing torpedo exploders and safer torpedo warheads.

Some of the most talented mechanical and chemical innovators of the period worked on these early automobile torpedoes. The pump-jet propulsion, electric propulsion, counter-rotating propellers, wire-guided control systems, improved body shapes, and gyro-controlled guidance systems are all concepts that ultimately became widely used in modern torpedoes.

7

The Whitehead Torpedo
Finally Joins the U.S. Navy

The U.S. Navy finally decided to evaluate the Whitehead automobile torpedo after learning of a successful Whitehead Torpedo attack during Chile's 1891 Civil War by a swift steam-powered gunboat on April 23, 1891, which sunk the 3,500-ton Chilean warship the *Blanco Encalada*. 300 crewmembers died. Some 26 years after introduction of the Whitehead Torpedo, U.S. experts finally got around to admitting to its value as an offensive weapon. Late in 1891, negotiations for torpedo-manufacturing rights in the United States began in earnest between the Navy, the Whitehead Company and the E. W. Bliss Company of Brooklyn, N.Y. Favorable terms were reached, and in 1892, the Navy contracted with Bliss for the manufacture of 100 Whitehead Mk 1 torpedoes at $2,000 each.

Between 1896 and 1904, the Bliss Co. manufactured approximately 300 additional Whitehead units of five types for the U.S. Navy. The 3.55-meter Mk 1, Mk 2, and Mk 3 torpedoes were the same, differing only in mechanical details. Both the Mk 1 and Mk 2 units were manufactured in the 5-meter length.

The performance of the two Mk 1 torpedoes was the same, but the 5-meter Mk 1 used the Obry steering gyro invented by the Austrian, Ludwig Obry, for azimuth control, and had the largest warhead of the torpedo of that time—220 pounds of wet guncotton.

The two Whitehead Mk 2 torpedoes differed in performance characteristics; the 5-meter versions had slightly better speed and nearly double the range of the 3.55-meter version. The significant difference between the Mk 3 and the other 3.55-meter Mk 2 did not have a gyro for control in azimuth.

The Whitehead Mk 3 was developed and produced in the 3.55-meter version only. The significant difference between the Mk 3 and the other 3.55-meter torpedoes was that it used the Obry steering gyro for azimuth control.

Initially, the Whiteheads had used a reciprocating engine in which the exhaust was expelled through a hole in the after body. This method of exhaust interfered with the torpedo steering. Peter Brotherhood (1838–1902), an engineer working for the Royal Laboratories at the Royal Arsenal, Woolwich, the British government-owned munitions works, developed a reciprocating engine, which exhausted into the crankcase, and then the exhaust was ducted to the tail of the torpedo through a hollow drive shaft. The Brotherhood engine along with counter rotating drive shafts developed by another Woolwich employee, possibly a Mr. Rendel, was adopted by Whitehead about 1880. This

Preparing a Whitehead Mk 3 for a practice launch.

innovation improved steering and eliminated the heel-and-roll tendency due to a single propeller.

Whitehead engines operated by compressed air classified as "cold running" torpedoes; those with air heaters were known as "hot running".

The advantage of hot gases for improving the efficiency was well understood, since unsuccessful attempts were made to heat the air in the air flask by burning a spray of liquid fuel in the air flask itself. These early attempts led to the use of an air heater also known as the combustion pot, and as a super-heater between the air flask and the engine. About 1901, Whitehead introduced the last model used by the U.S. Navy. The Whitehead Mk 5, a hot running torpedo used an air heater or combustion pot with kerosene as a fuel, and a four-cylinder reciprocating engine. The result of using heated air was remarkable. The Whitehead Mk 5 ran 4,000 yards at 27 knots, an increase in range by a factor of five. In this model, provision for varying the speed and range: 4,000 yards at 27 knots, 2,000 yards at 36 knots, and 1,000 yards at 40 knots. This varying speed and range accomplished by physically changing the reducing valve plug or varying its setting in the reducing valve, controlling the pressure/flow of the air and fuel to the combustion pot. The adjustment was made prior to tube loading through an access hole provided in the torpedo hull.

Exploder Mechanisms

All the early torpedoes employed a mechanical impact warhead detonating mechanism. These devices used percussion caps to initiate the detonation of the explosive train, and,

What appears to be a Whitehead Mk 3, developed in 1893 is shown exiting the firing tube from the deck of the Station's test firing pier.

The *Stiletto,* a speedy, wooden Herreshoff-built steam yacht, was purchased for the United States Navy under an Act of Congress dated March 3, 1887, and entered service in July 1887. Attached to the Naval Torpedo Station in Newport and later converted to an experimental torpedo boat, the *Stiletto* was the Navy's first torpedo boat capable of launching self-propelled torpedoes. Throughout her career the *Stiletto* was based at the Naval Torpedo Station. In this Official U.S. Navy photograph, the *Stiletto* is firing a Howell torpedo from her bow tube in the Sakonnet River, Little Compton, Rhode Island.

where used, the primers were dry guncotton placed bare in the primer exploder cavity prior to installation of the mechanism; "war nose" was the name given to the detonation mechanisms.

Prior to 1900, Whitehead Torpedo Works, Weymouth, England designed and manufactured war nose Mk 1. The war nose was mounted in the exploder cavity in the forward end of the warhead, on the longitudinal centerline of the torpedo.

A firing pin capable of longitudinal motion within the body of the war nose was held in place away from the percussion cap by a shear pin made of tin. Upon impact with the target, the shear pin broke and the firing pin would affect the percussion cap initiating detonation of the explosive.

To prevent accidental detonation during war nose installation, the war nose had a mechanical arming feature. A screw fan—propeller located on the forward end of the war nose, had to be rotated about 20 revolutions before the firing pin was free to move and influence the percussion cap.

War Nose Mk 2 Mod 0 was slightly larger than the Mk 1. It weighed 4½ pounds, was 6½ inches long and 3 inches in diameter, and had the same detonator as the Mk 1, but a primer of dry guncotton was also used to insure detonation of the warhead.

The principle advantage of the Mk 2 was that the war nose had four levers, known as whiskers, extending outward from the body casting which when struck, caused the firing pin to impact the detonator. War Nose Mk 2 Mod 1 was even larger, weighing 8 pounds, was 8 inches long, and 4 inches in diameter. The Mod 1 had longer whiskers and thus would fire on a glancing blow.

War Nose Mk 3 and Mk 4 never developed beyond the experimental stage. War Nose Mk 5 was the first warhead-detonating device for use in slow speed torpedoes designed to fire on impact from an angle or head on. The Mk 5, about 11 inches long, 2 inches diameter, and weighing about 5 pounds, employed a complicated firing mechanism that downgraded its reliability. These War Noses remained in use until 1911.

8

Torpedo Boats

Not that torpedoes had not existed before. Any infernal machine that would explode upon contact with the bottom or sides of a vessel—whether the contraption be floating free, anchored or arranged in layers in elaborate underwater timber structures and breastworks, in short, everything that might today pass as a marine mine—was up to the time of, and during, the [American] Civil War known by the generic term of torpedo. It was that kind of an "anchored torpedo" which Farragut damned when he gave his famous order at Mobile Bay. Not until the formerly stationary torpedo [received] a propelling mechanism which converted it, in Whitehead's own terminology, into an "automobile torpedo," did the need develop for a new type of craft that carried special apparatus through which the torpedo could be launched and started on its way to the target.

R. A. Shafter

Torpedo Boat Service

Before the reliability of the submarine torpedo boat was established, the preferred torpedo delivery platform was the speedy and stealthy surface torpedo boat. This vessel began life as a collection of pipes and tubes and steam boilers in a fragile steel enclosure that was a likely coffin for its sailors.

British-built Torpedo Boats

The most noted early nineteenth-century torpedo boat builders in Britain were the Thorneycroft Company and the Yarrow Company, both of London. These firms, each with a complement of 1,200 workers, built and sold their speedy steam-powered torpedo boats to many countries. The most remarkable element of the Thorneycroft boats was their exceptional speed. They could attain a sustained speed of 25½ mph. Yarrow's boats were only slightly slower at 24 mph. The British boats were constructed of steel in different classes ranging from 55-feet for harbor defense, to 166-feet, capable of extended cruises at sea.

Evolution of the U.S. Navy's Automobile Torpedo Firing Vessels

Here, we have Lieutenant W. S. Hughes' concise description of Admiral Dixon's *Alarm* and Captain John Ericsson's *Destroyer* torpedo boats.

Admiral David Dixon Porter's *Alarm*, was a vessel of a very novel type of torpedo boat employed for experimental purposes by the U.S. Navy. This vessel had the distinction of being the only boat of its kind in the U.S. Navy [c. 1885]. She was of iron construction, double hulled with several watertight compartments. By use of the Mallory steering propeller, she achieved great maneuverability; the Mallory is a rudder and propeller in one. Her design allowed use of either spar or automobile-torpedoes. This vessel combined the qualities of a gunboat, ram, and torpedo boat. The *Alarm's* statistics are 173-feet water line length, 27-feet 5-inches abeam, drawing 12-feet with an enormous underwater ram measuring 32-feet projecting from the bow. Within this hollow prow covered with 4½-inches of iron armor is the torpedo machinery. This consists of a cylindrical iron spar, 35-feet long carrying a torpedo to its outer end capable of running out under the water a distance of 25-feet ahead of the ram. Electric wires lead from the torpedo along the spar, through grooves to a firing trigger on deck.

Like the *Destroyer*, the *Alarm* is designed to fight "bows-on." The armament, in addition to the ram and torpedo, consists of one heavy gun mounted in the bow, for firing directly ahead, and a number of Hotchkiss and Gatling machine-guns. In action, it is intended that, simultaneously with ramming a hostile ship, the gun should be fired and the torpedo exploded.

Captain John Ericsson intended his submarine torpedo gun for installation in any class of vessel. However, his *Destroyer* was the only vessel then afloat that was adapted to such armament. Ericsson said his, "… submarine torpedo-gun may be applied to vessels of almost any class.…"

Lieutenant Hughes gives the following detailed description of Ericsson's *Destroyer,* a vessel that was a forerunner to the turn of the century monitor-class war ship.

The [*Destroyer*] vessel's lines are very sharp, and alike at both the bow and stern, thus enabling her to move ahead or astern with almost equal facility. The hull is 130 feet in length, built wholly of iron, partially armored at the bow; width, 17 feet; draught of water, 11 feet. Two iron decks, separated by a distance of about 3 feet, extend the whole length of the vessel, sheltering the crew and machinery, the space between the decks being filled with cork floats and bags of air to increase the buoyancy. A heavy iron shield, 2 feet thick, backed by 5 feet of solid timber, crosses the deck near the bow, inclining backward at an angle of 30 degrees, so as to deflect any shot that may strike it, below and behind which the crew, the gun, and all the vital parts of the machinery are situated. When equipped and ready for action, only a few inches of the *Destroyer* show above the water, thus exposing to an enemy but a small target, and at the same time affording to the crew and engines the additional protection of the surrounding water. The gun is discharged by electric wires leading to the pilothouse,

Bow view of David Dixon Porter's spar torpedo boat the *Alarm* in dry dock. *Photo courtesy the National Archives*

Stern view of Porter's *Alarm* showing the vessel's unusual Mallory steering propeller. *Photo courtesy the National Archives*

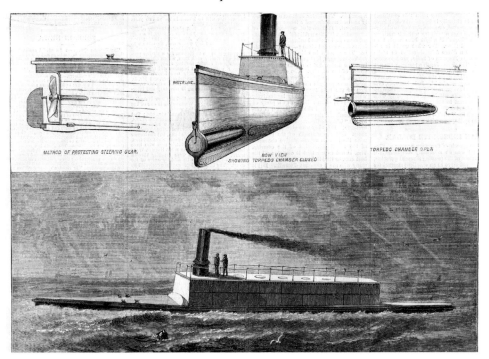

This vessel, built for the sole purpose of torpedo warfare, is the design of Captain John Ericsson. Ericson's *Destroyer* was reported to have great speed and excelled in her primary mission. Her armament was a submerged gun several feet below the waterline which fired a shell or torpedo containing 250 pounds of guncotton; the weapon's range is reported to be about 200 yards.

Ericsson's torpedo boat, the *Destroyer* at dockside appears as an ungainly vessel with a Whitehead torpedo on deck. *Photo courtesy the National Archives*

The deck of Ericsson's *Destroyer* reveals nothing of the inner working of this vessel. Built in 1890, she is certainly innovative for her three decks, each of which serves a specific function. The upper deck, shown in this photograph, carried two Whitehead-type torpedoes launched by hand. On the second deck, the so-called gun deck, she carried two additional torpedoes launched from firing tubes. Below these, the lowest deck carried Eriksson's experimental submarine gun, which was tested for Navy BuOrd without satisfactory results. Ericsson's Company sold the *Destroyer* to Brazil, but she was never placed in commission and her efficiency as a torpedo boat was never proven.

likewise situated behind the shield, where a reflector [periscope] affords the officer in command and the helmsman a full view of the horizon in front of the vessel.

The U.S. Navy's First Commissioned Torpedo Boats

The U.S. Navy's first especially commissioned experimental torpedo boat was reported in the May 4, 1889 issue of *Scientific American*.

In 1875, the Herreshoff Manufacturing Company of Bristol, Rhode Island received an order from the BuOrd to build a spar torpedo boat for the Naval Torpedo Station. This 58-foot wood vessel, called *Lightning* attained a sustained speed of 17¾ knots, with busts of 24 knots, which was a record speed at that time.

The greatest asset of all Herreshoff steamers was their boiler, in which steam was raised to working pressure in five minutes or less and could be kept at that pressure without difficulty. Herreshoff's speedy steamers steered just as well as well when going astern as when going ahead.

After 14 years of hard work at the Station, the *Lightning* worn out in her service was hauled ashore and scrapped.

The WTB-1 *Stiletto* steaming in Narragansett Bay with her full complement on deck, *c.* 1898.

The Stiletto

The U.S. Navy under an Act of Congress dated March 3, 1887 purchased the *Stiletto*, from the Herreshoff Manufacturing Co., of Bristol, Rhode Island for $25,000 and she entered service in July 1887; she was designated WTB No. 1 (Wooden Torpedo Boat), and assigned to the Naval Torpedo Station for automobile torpedo experiments.[2]

The *Stiletto*, a high boiler-pressure, single screw, vessel of 38.8-tons displacement sailed for many years as the Herreshoff brothers' personal steam-propelled yacht. The *Stiletto* distinguished herself as the swiftest steam-propelled yacht in American waters, racing against larger steamers, notably the *Mary Powell*, and winning handsomely.

When the Howell Mk 1 torpedo became a fleet weapon, the *Stiletto* was converted to fire these units by adding torpedo tubes and a steam-powered driver to spin-up the Howell's flywheel before firing. The *Stiletto* served to train personnel in the development of torpedo boat technology and tactics.

The *Stiletto* made the highest recorded speed for a boat of her length and displacement over a measured nautical mile, and had the highest recorded speed for a three-hour trial for a boat of her displacement, carrying a load of coal, water, crew, anchors and gear, and dead weight representing armament. The *Stiletto's* armament consists of Howell automobile torpedoes for attack, and for defense a Hotchkiss revolving cannon, hand grenades, and small arms. The Hotchkiss Ordnance Company of Providence, Rhode Island, manufactured the *Stiletto's* gun and torpedoes.

The original intention was to fit the boat with two bow torpedo tubes for shooting torpedoes forward, directly in line with the keel. This plan was abandoned in favor of having a torpedo gun mounted forward, on deck capable of training torpedoes discharged in any direction over 180 degrees. The following description is from the May 4, 1889 issue of *Scientific American*:

> The high efficiency realized by the *Lightning* and the *Stiletto* gives cause for belief that a new and larger steel torpedo boat, now building by the Herreshoff Manufacturing Company, under contract with the government, will yield results, which will do this enterprising firm credit when the time for her trial arrives. It is to be hoped that other boats may follow soon and that, while other nations are building by dozens and by scores, our government may see the wisdom of increasing these valuable adjuncts of naval force more rapidly than by occasional units.

Above: The sleek profile of the TB-1 *Cushing* the U.S. Navy's first all-steel, sea-going torpedo boat built in 1886 and commissioned in 1890, enjoyed a top speed of 22.5 knots. In this official U.S.N. photograph she is on her trial run without armament.

Below: In this photograph of *c.* 1898, the fully-armed *Cushing*, in her night-time camouflage paint exercises her crew in Narragansett Bay before departing to Florida waters where she will act as a courier during the war with Spain. *Cushing's* armament included three 6 pound rapid-fire guns and three 18 inch Whitehead torpedoes.

The Cushing

With the selection of the Howell torpedoes for fleet use, the Navy also initiated the design and procurement of a class of new steel-hulled fleet torpedo boats to employ the new weapons.

The Herreshoff boatyard was contracted to build the first of these vessels. The first of its class (TB-1) the U.S.S. *Cushing* was named in honor of the Civil War Hero Lieutenant William B. Cushing, who sank the Confederate ironclad warship *Albemarle* with a spar torpedo.

With the launching of the new 105-ton, 22.5-knot *Cushing* in January 1886, the Naval Torpedo Station became directly involved in supporting the fleet to get the new torpedo boats operational. This included installing and checking the weapon suite, providing training and support documentation, and firing a significant number of torpedoes to verify the operational effectiveness of the new torpedo boats. By the mid-1890s, the new *Cushing* class boats armed with three torpedo tubes firing Howell Mk 1 torpedoes were joining the fleet. During his command of the Torpedo Station, Lieutenant Commander F. French Fletcher (1902–1904) developed a new trainable torpedo tube that rotated to aim the torpedo at the target, which significantly increased tactical flexibility.

Harper's Weekly dated July 6, 1899 published this slightly inaccurate engraving of the TB 1 *Cushing*. In reality, the *Cushing* did not have port or starboard hull torpedo tubes. At a later date the vessel's sleek curved bow was transformed to a snub-nose with the addition of a center-bow-on torpedo tube. The upper right cartouche illustrates the *Cushing's* propeller and rudder; the lower left inset is a view of the Herreshoff boat yard from Bristol Harbor.

1. Seamen gunners, diving practice. 2. The testing dock. 3. Night attack by a torpedo boat under a search light in Newport Harbor. 4. Exploding a spar torpedo. 5. U.S. torpedo boat the *Cushing*. This illustrated page is from the January 4, 1896, *Harper's Weekly* magazine.

Crew of the torpedo boat TB14 *Morris* is loading a Howell torpedo into the boat's deck tube.

A grease-coated Howell torpedo is being eased into the aft tube of torpedo boat TB15 *Talbot*.

Above left: The torpedo boat TB4 *Morris* is launching Whitehead torpedo from its trainable firing tube.

Above right: The torpedo boat TB4 the *Rogers* is 160 feet water line length, 16 feet beam, and draws 5 feet; her top speed is 24½ knots. The *Rogers'* armament is three 18 inch Whitehead torpedoes and three 1 pounder rapid-fire guns.

The Herreshoff-built U.S.N. TB-7 *Dupont* displaced 165-tons; draft at 4.8-feet, waterline length 175-feet, armament four 1-pound rapid-fire guns and three 18-inch torpedoes; total cost to build in 1895, $144,000. In this 1898 photograph, the *Dupont* is in dry dock affording a unique view of the out-of-water size of the fully armed vessel.

The Navy purchased theTB-14 *Morris* from the Herreshoff Manufacturing Co. in 1886. The *Morris* at 105-tons, drew 4.1-feet, with a water line length of 138.25-feet, she had a top speed of 22 knots; her purchase price $144,000. Her armament included three 1-pound rapid fire guns and three 18-inch Whitehead torpedoes.

The 1895 Herreshoff-built TB-6 *Porter* is sister to the TB-7 *Dupont*; at the time, these two vessels were the largest of the Navy's sea-worthy torpedo boats with a top speed of 39-knots. Both of these vessels were in Cuban waters during the Spanish-American War.

The torpedo boat destroyer, DD11 *Perry* was laid down in April 1899 by the Union Iron Works, San Francisco; launched October 27, 1900 and commissioned September 1902. The weapon on deck appears to be a Whitehead Mk 5, developed by the Torpedo Station in 1901.

On 18 May 1897, the TB2 *Ericsson* arrived at the Torpedo Station, her homeport. Her builder was the Iowa Iron Works; she was a modified version of the *Cushing*. The *Ericsson's* waterline length was 149 feet 7 inches, beam 15 feet 5 inches, draft 4 feet 9 inches, she displaced 120 tons making a top speed of 214 knots. Her armament consisted of four 1 pound rapid-fire guns and three 18 inch torpedo tubes.

9

Submersible Torpedo Launching Platforms

Bushnell's Turtle and Fulton's Diving-boat the *Nautilus*

The first offensive attack by a boat especially designed to carry a torpedo was the inspiration of Connecticut Yankee Captain David Bushnell. Bushnell's invention accommodated one operator, who sat in a watertight compartment with enough air for about 30-minutes.

A quarter century passed before any further designs surfaced for a submersible torpedo boat. The celebrated American inventor Robert Fulton devised a diving-boat; putting his proposal to the French, and later the British Government, but both rejected him. Back in the States, Fulton met with so much opposition from the War Department and was so awkward in his presentations that he gave up his ideas of torpedo warfare and turned his attention to steam navigation.

J. H. L. Tuck and his Peacemaker

While Simon Lake and John P. Holland were experimenting with their submarine torpedo boats, Josiah Hamilton Llangdon Tuck began trials of his submersible torpedo boat, the *Peacemaker*, in New York Harbor, in 1885–1886. To take a dive in early experimental submarines was risky; many lives and machines were lost. It is important to remember that the submersible became operational before the invention of the periscope. Therefore, a fully submerged submarine was blind and directional navigation was usually calculating by dead reckoning. Open demonstrations of these clumsy-looking boats excited the curiosity of the public and the interest of Navy and Government officials.

> The *Peacemaker* is the name of a new submarine torpedo-boat designed by Professor J. H. L. Tuck, of New York. The boat is built of iron, thirty feet long, seven and a half feet broad, and six feet deep; she is driven by electricity. Professor Tuck has been twenty-two years perfecting the *Peacemaker*, and she has cost 16,000 dollars to build. Ordinarily, the top of the boat is not much above the surface of the water. By inverting 'fins' the boat can be driven entirely under water. By expelling air and letting in water as ballast, the boat can be sunk to any depth. The water can be expelled and its place taken by air in the, same manner. The

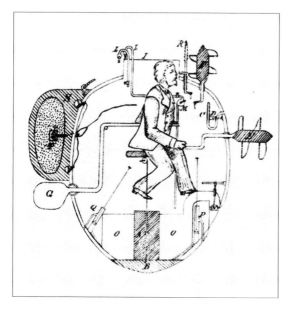

A reproduction sketch showing the basic workings of Bushnell's Turtle.

A cigar-shaped steamer believed to be a captured large-type Confederate *David* torpedo boat tied between two union monitors in Washington Navy Yard. *Courtesy U.S.N. Historical Photo Center*

vessel is steered by two rudders, whose planes are at right angles. The captain; acting also as steersman, clad in diver's dress; and, surrounded by water, stands in a well on the boat. In the interior of the boat that is lighted with incandescent lights and supplied with compressed air are the electrician and a man to attend to the air pumps. The captain signals the electrician to manage the boat and to discharge the torpedoes. The torpedoes, consisting of dynamite, are, made buoyant with cork. The boat, driven by electricity from storage batteries, runs up under a vessel, when the captain places the torpedoes, two in number, one on either side of the keel, and, being supplied with electric magnets, they cling to the bottom of the ship. Then the boat runs off, and at a safe distance, then torpedoes are exploded. Professor Tuck says the torpedoes can be attached to a vessel, which is going at the rate of ten knots an hour. When at anchor, the boat looks like a shark with a hole in its back.

Hawera & Normanby Star, December 11, 1884

John P. Holland

In 1875, John P. Holland, an Irish-born American cleric from Patterson, New Jersey, and engineer, built six submarines with private funding. In the Civil War Holland studied the Confederate's semi-submersible torpedo boat, the *David*. He had competing pioneering submarine inventors in Europe. However, thanks to his relentless experimentation, and a plethora of prototypes built throughout the 1880s, there finally emerged in 1895, the *Holland VII*, and in 1900, the *Holland VIII*.

The inventor cruised submerged in the Passaic River in his first submarine-boat, a slender, cigar-shaped vessel 16 feet long and 2 feet in diameter.

On January 14, 1896, Holland approached Captain George A. Converse, commanding officer of the Torpedo Station. He asked Converse to help convince the Navy Department and the Senate Committee on Naval Affairs to purchase six of his torpedo boats for $175,000 each.

Holland and his partner, the Electric Boat Company, had trouble convincing the Senate Committee that this new submarine torpedo boat was not experimental, but operational, and would be a good coastal defense vessel for the United States. Holland argued that his torpedo boat could be used, as a surface craft, as well as a submarine, which, he said, would make it more useful to the Navy.

The U.S.S. *Holland*

The Navy bought its first submarine on April 11, 1900. Designated SS-1 *Holland*, she came to the Naval Torpedo Station in Newport for demonstration and tests.

This *Holland* submarine torpedo boat, bought by the Navy, was the *Holland* VII, the final version in a long succession of prototypes produced since the 1880s. The technology involved in this submarine was the progenitor of every non-nuclear American submarine built until the 1980s. Holland's submersible vessel was a pressure hull surrounded by flooding ballast

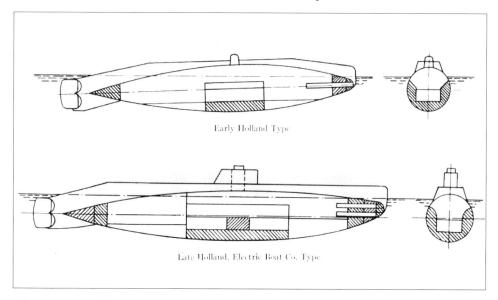

Schematic views of the original *Holland* and the later Electric Boat model.

The *Holland,* with crew on deck, arriving at the Brooklyn Navy Yard in October 1901.

tanks for submerging and resurfacing, an air-breathing engine for running on the surface, and electric motors for running submerged. She sported a bow torpedo tube; her length was 53 feet, her beam 10 feet, and she displaced 74 tons. Her armament included one Whitehead Torpedo tube, one aerial dynamite gun and an underwater dynamite gun.

In 1893, when Congress appropriated money for an experimental submarine, Holland won the competition, although the *Plunger* was to be Holland's seventh submarine, she was never finished. The Navy's *Holland* [SS-1] was the sixth of that name but she has become "*The Holland*" historically, the other submarines are mentioned only in marine histories or naval articles.

An article by Waldon Fawcett describing the early submarine the *U.S.S. Holland* originally appeared in the December 9, 1899 issue of *Scientific American*.

The success of the tests of the *Holland* submarine torpedo boat, recently made in the presence of an official trial board composed of United States navy officers at Peconic Bay on the north coast of Long Island marks the advent of a new era in the development of submarine craft designed for offensive warfare.

A number of the naval officers who witnessed the tests were favorably impressed with the performance of the boat, so impressed they believe that it is wise for the Navy Department to build or purchase a number of the vessels for service in harbor defense on both coasts.

The vessel was on several occasions under water for intervals of more than twenty minutes, and demonstrated her ability to respond to a summons to sink beneath the surface, approach a ship, discharge a torpedo, wheel about, and return to a place of safety, all within a space considerably less than half an hour.

The boat's tests were made at depths of about 20 feet, and demonstrated to the satisfaction of her builders and observers her ability to remain submerged for a span of 24 hours without any danger to the crew of six men. Based on the result of the experiments is a claim that the radius of action under water is five miles per hour for almost six hours.

Holland's boat is 53 feet in length by 11 feet in width; her weight is roughly 11 tons. The thoroughly insulated storage battery is in a compartment amidships, while over this is the conning tower with steering gear, and under it is the water tank. The air compressor and gasoline engine for driving the generator are located astern of the battery. Above is the dynamite torpedo tube. The generator may be either driven by the engine to charge the batteries or thrown on to the batteries, running as a motor while the boat is submerged. The motor generator weighs two tons, and is capable of developing 50 horsepower at 800 revolutions, or 150 horsepower at 1,200 revolutions. There are small motors for the pumps, the air compressor, and ventilating apparatus.

The American boat, since the recent trials, has attracted renewed attention from several foreign naval attachés stationed in the States, and some have sufficiently impressed to make the boat the subject of communications to their home governments.

The British Admiralty has always been strenuously opposed to submarine torpedo boats in general, and when the inventor of the American boat visited London, he was unable to interest them in the subject.

Opinions of Officers of the U.S. Navy were more thoroughly divided concerning the utility of the submarine boat in warfare. The personality of the men who have ranged themselves on opposite sides of the discussion makes it impossible to disregard the arguments of either. On the one hand, we have the advocates of this class of craft, who declare that its judicious employment would make it practically impossible for an enemy to attack successfully any of our principle seaports by sea. Opponents of submarine operations of the class proposed, base their claims of the impracticability of all submarine craft on the contention that the difficulty of keeping to a course when the boat is submerged would make it impossible to discharge torpedoes with any degree of accuracy.

Supplementing this latter argument is that of British engineers who assert those modern searchlights and other safe guards would insure the destruction of any submarine torpedo boat by rapid-fire guns before it could approach sufficiently near to a war ship to do any harm.

Lieutenant A. P. Niblack U.S.N., one of the best-informed officers on the subject of torpedo warfare in the American Navy, declared that there was no real reason why the submarine boat should not be as successful as the automobile torpedo'.

In 1900, the Navy's first submarine, the U.S.S. *Holland*, came to Newport for demonstrations and tests. In 1901, while carrying three Whitehead Mk 2 torpedoes, the *Holland* went through exercises with a Navy crew from the Torpedo Station. Lt. Harry H. Caldwell was in command, making Caldwell the Navy's first submarine captain. In exercises off the Newport shore, the *Holland* closed to within torpedo firing range of the U.S.S. *Kearsarge* without detection.

Other "A" type submarines such as the *Adder* and the *Moccasin* followed the *Holland*; these subs were equipped with a bow-mounted, 18-inch torpedo tube. During the infancy of the submarine torpedo boats, other classes had two or four 18-inch tubes installed and carried a total of four to eight torpedo weapons. The single exception was the G-3 class, which had six 18-inch torpedo tubes and carried a total complement of ten torpedoes. The preferred weapon for these early submarines was the Bliss-Leavitt Mk 7.

Beginning in 1918, all U.S. submarines, like America's surface Navy were retrofitted with 21-inch torpedo tubes. The 21-inch tubes fired Mk 10 torpedoes, which had the largest warhead of any torpedo of that time—500 pounds—with a speed of 36 knots, but a range of only 3,500 yards. The Torpedo Station developed the Mk 10 with assistance of the E. W. Bliss Co.

About 1910, the Bliss-Leavitt Torpedo Mk 9 came online around the same time as the Mk 10. The Mk 10 was intended to replace the Bliss-Leavitt Mk 3 on battleships. When the use of torpedoes in battleships was discontinued in 1922, the Mk 9 was converted for submarine use and was used in the early days of the Second World War, supplementing the limited inventory of Mk 14s.

Above: The U.S. Navy's first submarine torpedo boat, the *Holland*, in dry dock for maintenance at the Brooklyn Navy Yard. Totally exposed, the Holland's 53-foot overall length and 10-foot beam can be evaluated; her displacement was 74-tons.

Below: On January 14, 1896 John Holland, known as the father of the modern submarine, sent a letter to Torpedo Station Officer in Charge Captain George A. Converse. In the letter, Holland outlined the abilities of his submarine torpedo boat and asked Converse to convince the Navy Department and the Senate Committee on Naval Affairs to purchase six of his inventions at $175,000 each.

Holland and his partner the Electric Boat Company had reached out to the Senate Committee with their proposal, but were unsuccessful in making the sale. Eventually, after a series of successful sea trials witnessed by Government officials, the Navy purchased it first submarine on April 11, 1900.

In this 1903 photo, crewmen of the *Adder* warm up their engines at the Torpedo Station; a sister craft the *Moccasin* is moored astern. Both of these Holland-type submarines remained in service until 1922.

Bliss-Leavitt Mk 1, this weapon was developed in 1904. Increased air flask pressure and heated air service increased the MK 1's range to 4,000 yards at 27-knots.The Mk 1 remained in service until 1922.

Bliss-Leavitt and NTS developed the Mk 9 in 1915, for use on battleships; in this photograph the Mk 9 is on board the battleship U.S.S. *New York*. This torpedo was recalled and put in storage for later use on R- and S-class submarines.

The E.W. Bliss Co., developed the 18 foot Mk 4 torpedo in 1908; designed for use in submarines, early models were used on battleships and cruisers.

The U.S.S *Porpoise* (submarine #7, later SS-7), adjacent to U.S.S. *Shark* (submarine #8, later SS-8), 1903–1922, they were later renamed *A-6* and *A-7* respectively. The two 197 ton Plunger Class submarines were built at Elizabeth Port, New Jersey, and commissioned in September 1903.

The crew of the submarine *H-2* (SS-29) is hoisting aboard a spent Mk 4 practice torpedo during maneuvers off San Pedro, California.

The weekly *Scientific American* dated December 9, 1899 published this unusual stern view of the *Holland* from which we can study the submarine's propeller and rudder.

10

Other Surface Torpedo Launching Platforms

The Torpedo Joins the Fleet

With selection of the Howell as the Navy's first operational torpedo, the Naval Torpedo Station became increasingly committed to introducing automobile torpedoes to the fleet. This included not only the torpedo, but also all the related shipboard systems: launchers, storage, servicing, training of personnel, and logistic support. In 1900, the Naval Torpedo Station had 157 civilian employees, and as the torpedo related workload grew, it became increasingly difficult to support the other assigned experimental programs.

> Labor and material; general care of and repairs to grounds, buildings, and wharves; boats, instruction, instruments, tools, experiments and general torpedo outfits, eighty thousand dollars.
>
> For new machinery and tools for torpedo factory, fifty thousand dollars.
>
> For experimental work in the development of armor-piercing and other projectiles, fuses, powders, and high explosives, in connection with problems of the attack of armor with direct and inclined fire at various ranges, including the purchase of armor, powder, projectiles, and fuses for the above purposes, and of all necessary material and labor in connection therewith; and for other experimental work under the cognizance of the Bureau of Ordnance in connection with the development of ordnance material for the Navy, one hundred thousand dollars.
>
> *U.S. Navy Yearbook:* ACT August 22, 1912: Under the Bureau of Ordnance

Consistent with its established purpose, much of the production effort in the early days of the Torpedo Station was concentrated on manufacturing main charge explosive components compatible with specialized torpedo launching platforms.

The effort applied to torpedoes was in component development, ranging and acceptance of weapons manufactured by E. W. Bliss Co., coupled with experiments in launching torpedoes from various platforms. From the first, torpedo acceptance by the U.S. Navy was based on in-water performance.

Above and below: Pictured in the top illustration, crewmen are learning the proper technique of arming the so-called Berehaven boat mine. The casks hold a small electric battery trigger. The casks float on the surface attached to the plank—the charge hanging below. A vessel striking the plank explodes the charge. In the bottom illustration, "torpedomen" are fitting 72-pounds of guncotton into a mine, also fitted with an electrical device activated from the shore to explode the guncotton. These explosive devices are referred to as electro-contact mines. These photographs are from the British tabloid the *Navy and Army Illustrated*, dated August 20, 1897.

The TB-6 *Porter* is represented in this *Harper's Weekly* which shows officers and crew at drill. 1. Practice loading and aiming the torpedo; 2. Practice at the 1 pound rapid-fire gun; 3. Port view of the *Porter* firing a torpedo while underway; 4. The forward conning tower; 5. Sailors at work in the engine room; 6. The crew's cramped quarters; 7. Torpedo gunners practice placing a Whitehead torpedo in its launching carriage.

The New Navy

Starting in 1883, with authorization of the *Atlanta*, the *Boston*, the *Chicago*, and the *Dolphin* (the new steel ABCD ships) the Navy embarked on a major program to build a modern steel-hulled, steam-powered fleet. The world's other sea powers were already equipping their new armored warships to fire torpedoes. U.S. Naval authorities decided to follow suit.

The Naval Torpedo Station was directly involved in the installation, training, and maintenance of the new torpedo equipment for the ships. Initially the battleships were equipped with deck-mounted tubes firing Howell MK 1 torpedoes with steam-powered drives to spin-up the torpedo's flywheel before firing. These torpedo suites were not difficult to retrofit on ships already built.

When the Whitehead Torpedoes became generally available in the mid-1890s, some modification of the battleships became necessary, and an underwater bow-mounted tube added to fire the new weapons. As long as the fleet used the Howell and Whitehead Torpedoes, both types of tubes remained in the fleet. Some concern existed about launching torpedoes from the high deck tubes while the ship was maneuvering at high speed. This concern came about because during the Spanish-American War, at the Battle of Santiago, a torpedo on the deck of a Spanish warship exploded. Navy Command decided to standardize underwater tubes firing Whitehead Torpedoes for all capital ships and phase out the Howell MK 1 units.

Above left: *Frank Leslie's Illustrated Newspaper*, dated October 22, 1887, captions this full page graphic as "Our new Navy—experiments in assault and defense—attack of torpedo boats on the cruiser *Atlanta* in the Harbor of Newport, Rhode Island."

Above right: U.S.S. *Boston* was a protected cruiser and one of the first steel warships of the "New Navy" of the 1880s. Laid down on 15 November 1883 by John Roach & Sons, Chester, Pennsylvania, she was launched on 4 December 1884, and commissioned on 2 May 1887.

Spanish-American War

By the time the Spanish-American War began (1898), the U.S. Navy had 35 operational torpedo boats in service. Unfortunately, during the war, no opportunity arose for the new mosquito fleet to employ their torpedoes in combat. However, they did see extensive service blockading Cuban ports and serving as dispatch and patrol boats, and saw service shelling the enemy's shore installations.

In this conflict, the big guns of the capital ships remained the Navy's major weapon. Alas, the potential of the automobile torpedo was never proven.

Both admirals responsible for winning brilliant victories during the war were intimately familiar with the new torpedoes. Admiral Dewey had been the Executive Officer at the Torpedo Station during the early 1870s, and Admiral Sampson was the Naval Torpedo Station's Commanding Officer from 1884–1886.

The Torpedo Boat Destroyer

In 1895, Japanese torpedo boats attacked the Chinese fleet at anchor, sinking 14,000 tons. This action appears to have sparked the U.S. Navy's interest in developing a torpedo boat

A trainable torpedo launching tube on the Battleship *Maine* with a marine guard and a gunner. The original caption on this vintage photograph is: "The tube and its dangerous ammunition are continually under surveillance and their handling is committed only to experts."

On display are a Schwartzkopff torpedo and a bronze rifle surrendered to the U.S. Naval forces commanded by Commodore George Dewey by the Fort San Felipe (Cavite), Philippines, 1898.

countermeasure—the torpedo boat destroyer. The eventual development of this vessel was a larger and faster torpedo boat, the forerunner of today's Navy workhorse, the destroyer.

An article appearing in the November 11, 1899 issue of *Scientific American* sheds a bright light on these swift fighting vessels by the U.S. Navy.

> Thanks to the acts of Congress in the years 1896, 1897, and 1899, we either have now built or are building no less than thirty-seven torpedo boats and sixteen destroyers, fifty-three of these formidable little craft. At present, we have no torpedo-boat destroyers in commission in our Navy. The nearest approach to this type of vessel being built is boats such as the *Porter* and the *Dupont*, of 165-tons displacement and speed between 28 and 29 knots.
>
> There are other vessels much larger than these nearing completion, if not already commissioned, which while they would undoubtedly be capable of accompanying a fleet to sea and are as large as some of the torpedo boat destroyers in other navies, they are not listed as such in the official tables of the Bureau of Construction and Repair. Such are the 30-knot *Bailey* of 235 tons; *Farragut* of 273 tons, the *Goldsborough* of 247.5 tons, and the *Stringham*, of 340 tons which are expected to develop 30 knots with a total horsepower of 7,200.
>
> Nine of the destroyers are 420 tons displacement and they will develop speeds of 28 and 29 knots with 8,000 indicated horsepower. The names of these new ships are the *Bainbridge, Barry, Channery, Dale, Decatur, Paul Jones, Perry, Preble*, and the *Stewart*; being named for heroes whose names are associated with the most brilliant episodes of our naval history. It is noted that the three last named of these vessels, which are being built by the Union Iron Works, of San Francisco, are guaranteed to give a speed of 29 knots with 7,000 instead of 8,000 indicated horsepower. Each destroyer will carry on the main deck two torpedo tubes for discharge of the 18-inch Whitehead Torpedo. The armament will consist of two 12-pounder rapid-fire guns carried, one forward, and one aft, above the conning towers and protected by shields. There will be five 6-pounders carried in broadside on the main deck. These vessels will have a length of 245 feet, a beam of 23 feet 7½ inches, and a draught of 6 feet 6 inches.
>
> One excellent feature, which will give them considerable advantage over some of the latest boats constructed for foreign navies, is that in addition to their relatively large size they are provided with a long forecastle deck, which gives them an extreme freeboard, forward of 14 feet, the freeboard amidships being about 9 feet.
>
> These destroyers when completed cannot fail to produce a favorable impression. Their size, roominess, coal capacity, and powerful armaments, and above all their good sea-going qualities, and high speed, will place them in the front rank of this type of vessel.

The new class of offensive ship, the destroyer, also known as the torpedo boat catcher, needed two qualities: greater speed and heavier batteries than the torpedo boat. Initially, it was thought that the destroyer needed no torpedo tubes, but eventually it became a hybrid of the two types of ships: why build two classes of ships if one could undertake both functions. The destroyer began to be to be equipped with the torpedo tubes she had originally spurned, and so the prototype of the modern destroyer took shape.

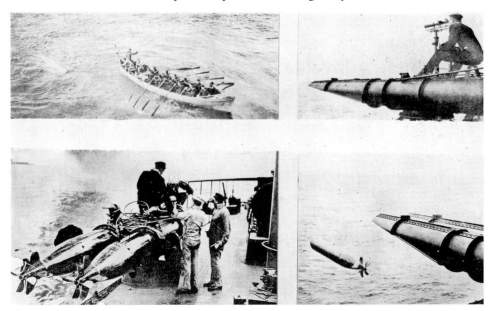

On the U.S. Navy's early torpedo boat destroyers the firing officer sat in a seat above clustered tubes with a sighting and range finding gear in front of him. He followed the distance and speed of his ship against that of the enemy ship greatly improving accuracy over dead-reckoning.

Torpedo Boat Destroyer No. 12, the *Preble* was laid down by the Union Iron Works, San Francisco, California on April 21, 1899; launched on March 2, 1901; and commissioned on December 14, 1903, Lt T. C. Fenton commanding.

The *Preble's* waterline length was 245 feet, beam 25 feet and drew 6½ feet; she displaced 420 tons and made 28.03 knots; her cost to build was $285,000. She was armed with the Torpedo Station's 1901 developed Whitehead Mk 5; this torpedo is similar in performance to the Bliss-Leavitt weapons of that era.

The first U.S.S. *Farragut* (Torpedo Boat No. 11/TB-11/Coast Torpedo Boat No. 5) was named for David Farragut, commander-in-chief of the U.S. Navy during the American Civil War. *Farragut* was launched 16 July 1898 by Union Iron Works, San Francisco, California and decommissioned 13 March 1919 and sold 9 September 1919.

Above: Distinguished guests on the deck of the torpedo boat *Porter,* view the trainable deck firing tube loaded with a Whitehead Mk 1 torpedo. In the background are the electrical, engineering and administrative buildings of the Naval Torpedo Station about 1900.

Below: The U.S.S. *Bainbridge*, Destroyer DD 1, a 420 ton vessel with a speed of 28 knots was the first of her class and the first ship classified as a destroyer by the U.S. Navy; she was built in Philadelphia, commissioned in November 1902 and remained in reserve status until February 1903 when she joined the North Atlantic fleet. Her armament consisted of two 3 inch 12 pounder and five 6 pounder rapid-fire guns, and two 18 inch Whitehead torpedoes. *Scientific American* graphic dated November 11, 1899.

Built by the Union Iron Works in 1896, the first of the U.S. Navy's new craft officially designated as a torpedo boat destroyer, the *Farragut*, of 279 tons with a speed of 31 knots, was launched July 16, 1898. Her armament consisted of four, 6-pound rapid-fire pompon guns and two, 18-inch torpedo tubes. Essentially, she was an oversized torpedo boat.

In 1898, the U.S. Navy observed the British Royal Navy's torpedo boat destroyer development program. Admiring their methods, the U.S. Navy ordered construction of four destroyer designs; as the class for the series, the 420-ton, 29-knot *Bainbridge* was selected. This distinctive class of destroyer with high forecastles started entering the fleet at the turn of the century.

The U.S.S. *Bainbridge*

The U.S.S. *Bainbridge* (DD 1), launched in 1901, was the first U.S. Navy torpedo boat destroyer— a few years later, ships of this type became known simply as destroyers. The *Bainbridge* displaced 420 tons; had a maximum speed of 29 knots, and was armed with 3-inch guns and two 18-inch torpedo tubes. These destroyers of torpedo boats were themselves torpedo boats as well. Shortly before the First World War in 1913, the Duncan class of 1,020 tons came into being. This class was equipped with 18 inch, double-or triple-mount torpedo tube firing the Bliss-Leavitt Mk 6 and Mk 7 torpedoes. Beginning with the U.S.S. *Caldwell* (DD 69) in 1917, the raised forecastle gave way to flush decks, displacement increased to 1,200 tons, and speed increased to 32 to 35 knots. Of far-reaching significance, the advent of the DD 69 also introduced the standard 21-inch surface torpedo tube. With tubes installed in triple mounts, four mounts per ship—12 tubes total. These ships fired the Bliss-Leavitt Mk 8, the U.S. Navy's first 21 inch by 21-foot torpedo with a range of 16,000 yards at a speed of 27 knots.

As seen in the accompanying photo of DD 1 *Bainbridge*, as on other early U.S.N. torpedo boat destroyers, the firing officer sat above the tubes with a sighting and range-finding gear in front of him. He allowed for the speed and course of his ship and for the enemy's. Firing is achieved by compressed air; the torpedo explodes upon striking the target when the detonator pin drives against a mechanism that ignites the charge of compressed guncotton. These artisan-made steel torpedoes, 21 inches in diameter, 17½ feet long, weighed more than one ton and cost about $7,500 each; each weapon could be set to travel at a fixed depth varying from zero to 25 feet, with a range of about 10,000 yards.

U.S.S. DD-1 *Bainbridge* is shown firing a Whitehead, Bliss-Leavitt Mk10 torpedo while underway; photograph is *c.* 1911.

Above: DD-14 the *Truxtun* was laid down on November 13, 1899 at Sparrows Point Maryland by the Maryland Steel Co.; she was launched on August 15, 1901, and commissioned on September 11, 1902.

Below: The "Gunners Gang" aboard the DD-14 *Truxtun* in San Diego. According to the note on this real photo postcard the torpedo is a 5 meter Mk 1 Whitehead. The writer's name is Arthur; he is the sailor in the photo holding a black cat—the ship's mascot.

11

The Bliss-Leavitt Torpedo and Station Development 1900–1910

About 1900, the British firm, Vickers, Ltd. who had licensed Whitehead's patents, revolutionized torpedo propulsion by devising an alcohol-burning "steam" torpedo powered by a small turbine. This innovation yielded higher speeds and much longer ranges.

At the turn of the century, Frank McDowell Leavitt, an engineer for the E. W. Bliss Co. [17 Adams Street, Brooklyn, N.Y.] developed a new turbine-powered torpedo that became the design base for U.S. torpedoes through the Second World War. Leavitt, an extremely talented designer, was the dean of U.S. torpedo designers, and the family of Bliss-Leavitt torpedoes that he designed introduced revolutionary new concepts including turbine power plant and hot gas combustion, establishing a design base that lasted for a half century. The Bliss-Leavitt Mark 4 torpedo also had gyroscopic control, and about one hundred of these units were purchased by the Navy for experimental purposes.

John Merrill and Lionel D. Wyld

In 1906, Admiral N. E. Mason, Chief of the Bureau of Ordnance, petitioned Congress for a torpedo appropriation of $500,000; Mason earmarked $150,000 of the appropriation to establish a U.S. Navy Torpedo Factory on Goat Island. When granted, the Navy sent Lt-Cdr Gleaves and Lt-Cdr Davidson to the Vickers-Armstrong torpedo factory in England to study the manufacturing process of Whitehead Torpedoes.

Following the Gleaves and Davidson study, and concerned about security, the Navy became very upset when Bliss attempted to sell their new turbine-powered hot-gas torpedo to foreign countries. To ensure the security of future torpedo designs, in 1907, the U.S. Navy built a factory at the Torpedo Station specifically to produce an American version of the British weapon. Estimated annual factory production was 100 torpedoes with spare parts, and to support this effort, a major reorganization was required. Chief Clerk J. P. Sullivan became director of administrative reorganization, and Quartermaster John Moore set up the machinery and artisan workforce.

In January 1908, before the factory was completed, the Torpedo Station received its first order to manufacture 20 18-inch Mk 5 Whitehead Torpedoes incorporating the new hot gas design powered by four-cylinder radial engines. These weapons were the first

In 1904, engineer Frank Leavitt developed a turbine-driven anti-surface-ship torpedo which was designated the Bliss-Leavitt Torpedo Mk 1. The use of increased air flask pressure and heated air increased the range of the Mk 1 to 4,000 yards at 27 knots. This weapon served on battleships, torpedo boats, and cruisers.

One hundred Whitehead Mk 3 torpedoes were purchased from the E. W. Bliss Co. and in 1913, this weapon was later designated Torpedo Type A. Developed in 1893, it was withdrawn from service in 1922 when all torpedoes designed prior to torpedo Mk 7 were decommissioned in favor of weapons that were more modern.

multi-speed (27, 36, and 40 knots) vehicles issued to the fleet. The 40-knot vehicles had a 4,000-yard range.

In the summer of 1908, the new factory was completed. Soon, additional space was needed for a foundry, pattern shop, and a forge. The Torpedo Station instituted an extensive expansion program to move the power plant close to the electrical laboratory, and level the remnants of old Fort Wolcott to free an area on the west side of the island for industrial growth.

Adding their own improvements—notably injecting water into the combustion chamber for more steam—Torpedo Station engineers scaled the resulting Bliss-Leavitt torpedo up to 21-inch diameter to yield a weapon that could travel at 36 knots to a range of 3,500 yards. This was designated torpedo Mk 10, and more than 1,000 were built for use in the First World War. The Torpedo Station dramatically expanded its manufacturing capacity for the war.

By 1910, the Torpedo Station employed 445 civilian workers, the torpedo factory was in full production, and orders for more than 100 Whitehead Torpedoes were on the books. By September 1912, the initial 20 Mk 5 torpedoes were delivered from the U.S. Navy's first operational in-house torpedo factory. During these early years, approximately 500 Mk 5 Whitehead Torpedoes rolled off the production line. Such was the demand that immediately upon completion of the original factory a second factory was under consideration at the Goat Island site.

Getting the new torpedo factory built and operational was the priority task during the first decade of the twentieth century. The Station was also involved in conducting basic research: developing new weapon concepts; and providing technical support to the fleet. Training continued with both officers and enlisted men instructed in a wide range of formal classes including torpedoes, diving, guns and gun control systems, mines, printing, torpedo boat and submarine operations, countermining and other subjects.

Bliss-Leavitt continued to develop new turbine-powered torpedoes. By 1910, a new 18-inch- diameter by 204-inch-long torpedo with a horizontal contra-rotation turbine for destroyer use, with a speed of 35 knots, and a 2,000 yard range, was developed and designated as the Bliss-Leavitt Mk 6 torpedo. Fewer than 100 of these torpedoes were produced for fleet use before Bliss-Leavitt introduced an improved model of increased performance.

Existing hot gas torpedoes were run fuel-lean to maintain combustion temperature at approximately 1,000° F, which kept the turbine wheels from melting—consequently, the full thermodynamic energy available was not used. A new concept was burning fuel and air at near the correct stoichiometric mixture by introducing water into the combustion chamber. The water flashed into steam, thereby reducing the temperature and at the same time substantially increasing masses of gas driving the turbine wheels. Bliss-Leavitt and the Torpedo Station used this new combustion system in the Bliss-Leavitt Mk 7. Because the new system used water as a diluent to suppress the combustion temperature, the Mk 7 torpedo was erroneously referred to as a "steam" torpedo.

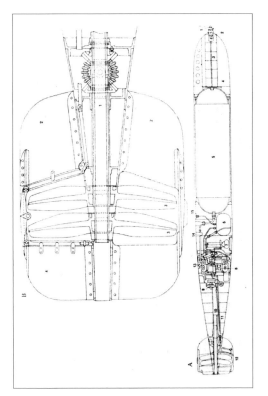 

Above left: In this Torpedo Station engineering schematic drawing the inner workings and details of the tail assembly of the Bliss-Leavitt Whitehead torpedo are revealed.

Above right: Crewmen are hauling aboard a Bliss-Leavitt Mk 6 torpedo after a practice war-shot. *Photo postcard dated 1911*

Although the performance of torpedoes had been increasing dramatically, the revolutionary new British Dreadnought battleship, introduced in 1906, extended ship gun ranges to 10,000 yards. This mandated an urgent need for long-range, high-performance torpedoes to counter the new battleships. One solution was to increase the size of destroyer torpedoes, and in 1911 development of the 21-inch diameter by 256-inch-long turbine-powered Mk 8 torpedo came about. The Mk 8 was essentially a scaled-up version of the Mk 7 torpedo. Raising air flask pressure from 2,250 psi to 2,800 psi, the warhead from 281 pounds to 466 pounds and the speed to 36 knots with a range of 16,000 yards affected the weapon's deadliness. The torpedoes were ideal for the flush decks of the new Clemson/Wilkes class destroyers, and were employed extensively by torpedo boats during the First World War. The UK deployed more than 600 Mk 8 torpedoes for use on 50 of its First World War-era destroyers. Volume manufacture of the Mk 8 torpedoes was continued during the First World War on Goat Island, the Naval Gun Factory in Washington, DC, and the new torpedo plant in Alexandria, Virginia, which continued in use until the Second World War.

U.S.S. *Wickes*. The Wickes-class destroyers were a class of 111 destroyers built by the U.S. Navy in 1917–19. Along with the 6 preceding Caldwell-class and 156 subsequent Clemson-class destroyers, they formed the "flush-deck" type. Only a few were completed in time to serve in the First World War, including U.S.S. *Wickes*, the lead ship of the class.

DD296, U.S.S. *Chauncey*, one of the fifth batch of Clemson class destroyers, commissioned in 1919. She was a casualty of the Honda Point disaster, the largest peacetime loss of U.S. Navy ships. On the evening of September 8, 1923, seven destroyers, while traveling at 20 knots ran aground at Honda Point, a few miles from the northern side of the Santa Barbara Channel off Point Arguello on the coast in Santa Barbara County, California. Two other ships grounded, but were able to maneuver free of the rocks. Twenty-three sailors died in the disaster.

High Performance Torpedo

With the new high performance Mk 8 destroyer torpedo in production, the Torpedo Station was under pressure to develop more of the same type for use on battleships and submarines. The Navy therefore authorized a new Mk 9 battleship torpedo, and design and development studies began. One stipulation was that the new torpedo fit into existing 21-inch torpedo tubes previously used for the Bliss-Leavitt Mk 2 and Mk 3 torpedoes; this effectively limited the length of the new torpedo to less than 200 inches.

During development of the Mk 9 torpedo, range was considered more important than warhead size and speed for battleship use. The E. W. Bliss Company and the Torpedo Station developed the Mk 9 battleship torpedo jointly; it was 21 inches in diameter, 197 inches long, had a speed of 27 knots, and carried a 210-pound warhead a distance of 7,000 yards. The speed and warhead of the new torpedo were approximately the same size as those of the Mk 3 torpedo it replaced, but the range had almost doubled. Development of the Mk 9 ended just before the First World War, and in May 1914, the Torpedo Station built 200 of these battleship torpedoes.

During the same period in which engineers developed the Mk 9 torpedo for use on battleships, the Navy decided on the production of a larger high-performance torpedo for submarines. A new 21-inch diameter, 195-inch-long Mk 10 torpedo was developed that incorporated the same basic Bliss-Leavitt technology used in designing the Mks 8 and 9 torpedoes; and again, a design tradeoff was made. Strategists assumed that use of submarines in torpedo attacks against capital ships would be at close range and therefore long range was substituted for larger warhead. The Mk 10 had a 497-pound warhead, the largest torpedo warhead to date. Its speed was 36 knots and its range was only 3,500 yards. The new Mk 10 torpedoes, continued in service into the early years of the Second World War.

The Mks 9 and 10 torpedoes completed a family of 18-inch and 21-inch diameter Bliss-Leavitt "steam" torpedoes used on submarines, torpedo boats, destroyers, cruisers, and battleships.

12

Events Leading to
the First World War

The Battle at Tsushima

A major sea battle involving fleets employing torpedoes and destroyers for the first time came during the Russo-Japanese War at Tsushima in May 1905. Admiral Togo's Imperial Japanese Fleet annihilated Admiral Rozhestvensky's Second Pacific Squadron in a classic big ship clash. Once the Russian battle line was broken, Togo aggressively used his destroyers to mount torpedo attacks against single Russian warships. At nightfall, the Russians attempted to disengage and escape to Vladivostok, but the Japanese destroyers continued to pursue them, inflicting substantial damage. During the battle, more than 370 torpedoes were fired, conclusively demonstrating that torpedo-armed destroyers could be a significant factor in a major fleet engagement.

Lessons learned from the battle at Tsushima by the world's major naval powers—the Americans, British, French, and Germans—encouraged improvements to their destroyers, including arming them with superior long-range torpedoes.

Towards the end of the nineteenth century, the torpedo had a profound impact on the evolution of warships and the development of tactics. The U.S. Navy installed torpedo tubes on all types of warships, from battleships to small steam launches, and shore-mounted torpedo batteries for harbor defense. Double-hulled ships with extensive compartmentalization protected big ships from the torpedo's underwater warhead explosion, and small high-speed torpedo boat catchers operated along with the battle fleet in defending against torpedo boat attacks. By the turn of the century, combining the best features of torpedo boats and torpedo boat chasers provided the design base for a new generation of nimble, multifunctional, torpedo-armed platforms that later became known simply as destroyers.

The fast, agile and maneuverable destroyer provided the fleet with a new offensive capability, and ultimately this new class of warship became the workhorse of the Navy. As an indispensable part of battle fleets, they provided defense against enemy torpedo attacks and the offensive ability to conduct massed torpedo attacks against an enemy fleet. Destroyers were also used as scouts to lay smoke screens and, later, to protect the fleet from submarine attacks. The battle at Tsushima had demonstrated the wisdom of this policy.

The Arms Race and Preparations

As the great armaments race in Europe intensified just before the First World War, the United States responded by committing additional resources to national defense. In 1907, the Bureau of Ordnance allotted $155,000 for the erection of the Federal Government's first torpedo factory on Goat Island. The new factory, designed to manufacture 50 torpedoes per year, began operations in the summer of 1908. The number of employees at the Station increased from 185 in 1908 to 625 in 1914.

Although getting the new torpedo factory built and operational was the priority task during the first decade of the twentieth century, the Naval Torpedo Station was also involved in conducting basic research, developing new weapon concepts; providing technical support to the fleet; and conducting various formal classes—training fleet personnel in torpedoes, guns, mines, and other technical ordnance.

The Station was also involved in the development and production of explosive devices. Tests were conducted on the Davis projectile torpedo, also known as the Davis torpedo

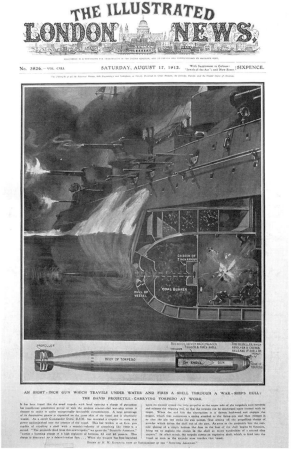

An illustration and description of the Davis Torpedo from the *Illustrated London News,* August 17, 1912.

gun, designed to penetrate the heavy armor plate of new battleships. This new weapon consisted of a standard torpedo with the warhead replaced by a large armor-piercing shell with an explosive charge that fired the projectile through the ship's armor plate before exploding. The Station also expanded its efforts in mine development. Although the manufacture of naval defense mines transferred to Philadelphia and Norfolk in 1915, the Station remained actively involved in new mine development to the end of the First World War. Experiments were conducted to develop small charges that could countermine torpedoes while approaching a ship. The same experimental program was used to design and evaluate a new generation of countermine resistant torpedo exploders.

The Station developed and evaluated the design of steel nets to protect anchored ships from surprise attacks, while simultaneously developing net cutter torpedo heads to penetrate these nets.

The Torpedo Station production capacity increased significantly through the years. In 1913, annual production was approximately 100 torpedoes. When the new factory, assembly shop, and storehouse built in 1915, became operational, the single-shift capacity increased to 300 torpedoes per year. Just after the war ended in 1919, 1,312 Mk 10 torpedoes were under construction on Goat Island.

The Naval Torpedo Station had morphed into a major industrial complex, enlarging the forge shop, acquiring a test barge and building a new foundry, incinerator, and a large concrete storehouse. Additionally, railroad tracks were laid allowing flatcars to move torpedoes, mines, and supplies between buildings. Goat Island looked less like a naval base, and more like a giant industrial site.

A test firing at the Station.

Above: All torpedo-handling personnel are on deck to learn the number of "kills" scored during target practice.

Left: Governors of several states are observing a torpedo boat and destroyer flotilla review in Narragansett Bay.

13

The First World War

The German U-boat threat

By the spring of 1917, when the U.S. entered the First World War, the German U-boat threat was so great that it overshadowed all other wartime dangers. Torpedo research and development slowed in favor of further developing depth charges, and depth bombs, (depth charges appropriate for dropping from aircraft) in addition to mines, which were the antisubmarine warfare weapons of that era. The Naval Torpedo Station redirected its resources and played an important role in further developing the depth charge, which supplanted the British depth charge design.[6]

Use of the torpedo by the U.S. Navy and Allies in the First World War was not a major factor in any naval fighting; conversely, German submarines are credited with sinking 5,408 ships for a total tonnage of 11,189,000.

When the United States became directly involved in the First World War, Navy destroyers and submarines were deployed in Europe, and an urgent need arose for forward bases and facilities to support the U.S. Navy ships operating in foreign waters. In support of this requirement, the Naval Torpedo Station built a complete torpedo workshop, designated Advance Base No. 6. Lieutenant Commander Radford Moses headed the workshop in Queenstown, Ireland, which provided torpedo assembly for U.S. Navy ships. Additionally, the Station provided torpedo outfits to the many newly commissioned ships, and torpedo retrofit kits to ships already operational before going to the war zone.

Despite all the preparations by the Station, the Navy did not have any opportunities to fire warshot torpedoes or conduct any major fleet actions during the First World War. The German Navy had remained chiefly secure in its home anchorage. Both the Germans and the British conducted extensive torpedo firings during the war, which gave both countries the opportunity to discover and correct weapon problems. Unknown to the U.S. Navy, its torpedoes also shared some of these basic exploder and depth-keeping problems. The Navy discovered this problem only after the war when it began firing significant numbers of its warshot torpedoes.

The Naval Torpedo Station and the E. W. Bliss Company had developed the Bliss-Leavitt torpedo Mk 9 around 1915. Torpedo production for the U.S. Navy was terminated by the Bliss Company about 1920 after completion of the Mk 9 project.

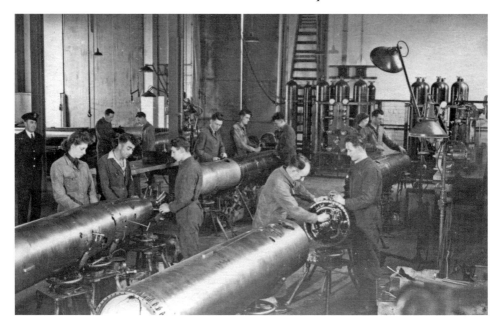

When the United States became directly involved in the First World War, Navy destroyers and submarines were deployed in Europe. To support U.S. Navy ships operating in foreign waters the Naval Torpedo Station built a complete torpedo workshop in Queensland, Ireland.

In the Mk 9 torpedo, warhead size and speed were sacrificed for increased range, considered an important factor for battleship use. The Mk 9 battleship torpedo was 21-inched diameter by 187-inches in length, its range 7,000-yards at a speed of 27-knots with a 210-pound warhead. The speed and warhead size of this new vehicle were approximately the same as those of the Mk 3 torpedo it was replacing, but the range had almost doubled. In May 1914, NTS was ordered to manufacture 200 of these new torpedoes.

At the same time as the Mk 9 torpedo was in development for battleships, the Navy decided a larger high-performance torpedo should be produced for submarine use. As a result, a new 21-inch-diameter,195-inch-long Mk 10 torpedo was developed that incorporated the same Bliss-Leavitt technology used in the Mks 8 and 9 torpedoes, but once more a design tradeoff was made. The Navy assumed submarines would attack battleships at close range using torpedoes, so range was traded off for payload.

The Mk 10 had a fearsome 497-pound warhead, the largest of any torpedo up to that time. Its speed was 36 knots but its range only 3,500 yards. The new Mk 10 torpedoes, designed for use in the new R&S class submarines built during the First World War, continued in service until early in the Second World War.

The Mk 9 and Mk 10 torpedoes, the last fleet torpedoes developed before the First World War, completed a family of 18-inch and 21-inch diameter Bliss Leavitt steam torpedoes used on submarines, torpedo boats, destroyers, cruisers, and battleships. When the First World War began, emphasis at the Station was placed on production

The Bliss-Leavitt Mk 9 on board the BB-36 *Nevada*. U.S.S. *Nevada* was launched in July 1914; of 27,500 tons and 583 feet in length, carrying ten 14 inch guns, and twenty-one 5 inch guns, she was the only battleship to get underway during the attack on Pearl Harbor. Her complement of submerged 18 inch torpedo tubes was two or four—the exact number is unknown.

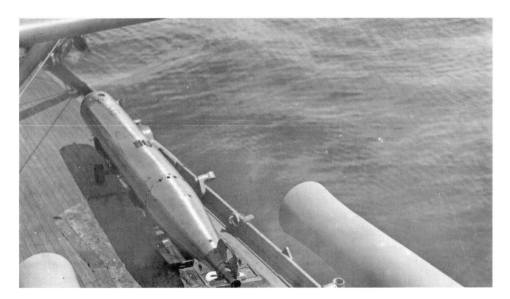

Above: A Bliss-Leavitt Mk 9 rests on the deck of the BB-25 *New Hampshire*. The 16,000 ton *New Hampshire* was launched on June 30, 1906; her armament includes four 21 inch torpedo tubes.

Right: Hauling aboard a spent Bliss-Leavitt Mk 9 after torpedo target practice.

and the facilities continued to expand. In 1917 when American involvement on the war seemed imminent, operations geared up to three eight-hour work shifts and the workforce enlarged until it numbered 3,200 employees. The Station's primer production exceeded 200,000 per year during the war years.

The Station's production capacity significantly increased through the years. In 1913, just before the war, only 100 torpedoes were being produced annually. When the new factory came on line in 1915, the single eight-hour shift production increased to 300 units per year, by war's end in 1919, 1,312 Mk 10 torpedoes were being built. In addition to manufacturing torpedoes, the Station continued to be responsible for proof-firing new weapons, certifying their readiness for fleet delivery, and issuing warshot torpedoes to the fleet.

In 1913, a torpedo-testing barge was added to the Station's floating test equipment with above-water test firing tubes, a training room, a small machine shop, and a large living space for seaman gunners under instruction. In 1917, as the tempo of war increased, a second fully equipped torpedo-testing barge came on line.

Worker Safety

A new deep diving training school was built at the Station with a pressure tank simulating deep ocean depths. On May 8, 1918, Petty Officer Frederick Reif lost his life while diving in the new training tank.

On January 26, 1918, the risk of working with highly volatile explosives was dramatically demonstrated when an explosion destroyed three primer storehouses and severely damaged a fourth; twelve men were killed and seven received serious burns. A few months later, on May 24, 1918, a powder flare in the primer room injured several men and two lost their lives.

These deadly accidents caused justified concern about the large amounts of explosives stored at the Station located in Newport Harbor only a few hundred yards from the densely populated downtown section of the city. To meet this concern, in 1919, the Navy purchased Gould Island located off Coddington Cove in Middletown, Rhode Island. This remote site became the facility for volatile warhead storage. Later, the Station acquired several acres of property on the Coddington Cove shore adjacent to Gould Island that became known as the Torpedo Station Annex.

Growth of the Island During the War

When the Navy took over Goat Island in 1869, it consisted of 10 acres of land. By the end of the First World War, the size of the island had doubled. This growth came from building sea walls, dumping ashes from the heating and power plants, and construction of docks and piers. Despite this dramatic increase in size, Goat Island was very crowded, and some of the more dangerous operations needed relocation to more remote sites.

The Naval Torpedo Station in the War Effort

The Station continued direct support of the fleet by installing torpedo suites. For instance, in 1913, fifteen new ships were provided with operational torpedo outfits, and 106 torpedoes were issued to these new ships. Additionally, another eleven ships had their torpedo suites modernized and 82 new steam torpedoes were issued to those ships.

Despite the war, training remained a major function at the Station. The facilities strained as war clouds darkened and thousands of civilians began volunteering for naval service. These raw recruits needed training in the operation of naval weapons.

When the United States entered the war in 1917, most torpedoes fired by German U-boats were used to sink ships carrying supplies urgently needed by the European Allies. This aggressive "unrestricted submarine warfare" tactic against unarmed merchant vessels came as a surprise. A grave need arose for new weapons and techniques to counter this potent terror. The problem of defending Allied ships from torpedo attacks became the nation's highest priority, and the Station under the direction of Chester T. Minkler received orders to use its technical expertise in torpedo warfare to develop a system of anti-submarine warfare (ASW) tactics, techniques, and weapons. With this unique assignment, the Station became the Navy's first ASW research and development (R&D) facility.

The British had developed a primitive depth charge to drop on submerged submarines, but it was discovered that the bomb's depth-sensitive fuse was unreliable. The bombs could prematurely explode, making them a danger to the vessel that dropped

Lowering a 21-inch torpedo in the fore-hold © N. Moser, N.Y.

A 21-inch Mk 9 torpedo is being loaded into the fore-hold of a First World War battleship.

them. Minkler, in a remarkably short time, designed a new improved depth charge that became known as an "ash can." The British, impressed, recommended immediate volume production of the weapon. The Station was fully committed to the production of torpedoes, so the manufacturing of the new depth charges was contracted out to private industry. This new weapon played a major role in the campaign to counter U-boats during the First World War; 72,000 were ordered and more than 40,000 were issued for fleet use.

The Station continued experimenting with the towed depth charge for ASW, developing the "aero bomb" for use against ships and submarines, and continued developing a new family of mines. Although the manufacture and assembly of naval defense mines had transferred from the Station to other naval activities prior to the First World War to free-up production facilities, the Station still had the responsibility for the development of new mines. Minkler designed and patented "horn" fuses that set off the classic bottom-moored mines used for harbor defense.

The new Mk VI moored mine incorporating creative new features was initiated in June 1917, and deployed for service use by February 1918. Notably, thousands of these mass-produced mines were seeded in the North Sea mine barrier, preventing German U-boats from sailing out of German harbors into the North Sea.

The Torpedo Station grew dramatically during the First World War, providing resident expertise and facilities required to respond to the Navy's urgent wartime operational needs. It is undeniable that the Naval Torpedo Station in Newport Harbor played a major role in bringing the German U-boat campaign under control.

14

Between the Wars

After the War

After the armistice, there was a worldwide reduction in naval armament, which during the 1920s resulted in a wave of cuts in military spending. Funding for torpedo research and development reduced with an allocation of only $30,000 per year for the Torpedo Station in Newport.

Although the Station received warm praise for its important contributions in support of the Navy's wartime requirements, it also attracted criticism from some quarters, for neglecting new torpedo development as it focused on the aero bomb, depth charges, and mine development programs.

By the end of the First World War, the torpedo was firmly established as a major new naval weapon capable of inflicting immense damage. The torpedo's significant impact at both tactical and strategic levels proved that self-propelled torpedoes would play major roles in modern naval warfare.

The Washington Naval Conference, 1921–1922

The major powers who had won the First World War, the Britain, France, Italy the USA and Japan, convened in Washington in November 1921 to negotiate an arms reduction treaty. Defeated Germany was not included.

From the viewpoint of those supporting the idea of a strong United States Navy, the Washington Conference was a disaster. Of equal significance, however, was the failure of Congress to appropriate sufficient funds to bring the Navy up to treaty strength and its unwillingness to spend funds on the development of new weapons systems during the interwar period. Such constraints may have frustrated naval officers, but they were quite compatible with public opinion, variously influenced by pacifist propaganda, economic developments, stubborn proponents of antiquated strategy and tactics and the lobbying of prophets of aerial warfare.

World leaders take a stroll during a recess at the World Disarmament Conference in Washington, DC, in November 1921. Secretary of State Charles Evans Hughes is at the center. *Library of Congress Prints and Photographs Division*

The Station in the 1920s and 1930s

Because the Naval Torpedo Station had a record of accomplishment and fifteen years' experience making torpedoes, it was considered capable of providing for all of the Navy's immediate needs. At the same time, torpedo production at the Washington Navy Yard and the Naval Torpedo Station in Alexandria, Virginia halted. The Newport Torpedo Station became the headquarters for all things torpedo related: encompassing research, development, design, manufacture, overhaul, and ranging.

In a new move to reduce maintenance costs, in 1922, all stockpiled torpedoes made prior to the Bliss-Leavitt Mk 7 were withdrawn from service and scrapped in favor of modern torpedoes. With this move, the U.S. Navy inventory of torpedo model types consisted of four:

1   Torpedo Mk 7 for destroyers and submarines with 18-inch tubes,
2   Torpedo Mk 8 converted for use with 21-inch submarine tubes,
3   Torpedo Mk 9 converted for use with 21-inch submarine tubes, and
4   Torpedo Mk 10 used by submarines with 21-inch tubes.

In the mid-1920s, production was minimal, and efforts were principally concerned with improving existing torpedo inventory. Torpedo Mk 11, which began life at the Washington Navy Yard, was completed at the Goat Island facility in 1926. The intended use of the Mk

Recovering a practice Bliss-Leavitt Mk 9 to the U.S.S. *Utah* during training in the 1920s.

11 was for installation aboard destroyers and cruisers, a formidable weapon; the Mk 11 had multi-range and speed selections. Production of the Mk 11 began in 1927 and ended in 1928, with about 200 Mk 11s produced; the reason was the introduction of the Mk 12. The use of torpedoes on cruisers ended in 1936.

The 1930s saw the development and production years for the Mk 13 aircraft torpedo, the Mk 14 submarine torpedo, and the Mk 15 destroyer torpedo. These "modern" torpedoes constituted the U.S. Navy's inventory at the start of the Second World War. The Mk 14 was described as follows:

> Torpedo Mk 14 has the ability for straight or angle running. Target fire-control data is introduced electrically through cabling between the torpedo tube door and the two-speed servo motor synchro-transmitter system in the torpedo. During launch, this cable is severed and the torpedo runs at the preset gyro-angle and depth.
>
> The power plant consists of two turbine wheels driven by hot gases and steam is generated by burning alcohol in a combustion chamber. The turbines drive two counter-rotating propellers, which prevent heel and roll. As the torpedo is impulse-fired from the tube, the propulsion system starts mechanically with an air-initiated igniter. During its run, an air-driven gyroscope and reciprocation steering engine control the course of the torpedo in azimuth. A pendulum and a hydrostatic diaphragm control the running depth.
>
> The four main sections of the torpedo consist of the head (war or exercise), the air flask (containing high-pressure air, fuel, and water for propulsion and steering), the after body

Developed by the Naval Torpedo Station, the Mk 13 was the first U.S. Navy torpedo designed specifically for aircraft launch.

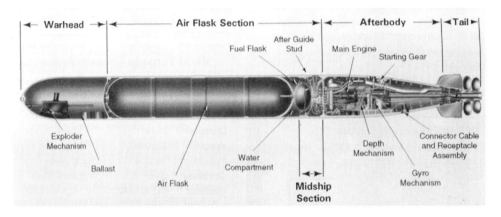

| ◄ Warhead ► | ◄ Air Flask Section ► | ◄ Afterbody ► | ◄ Tail ► |

After Guide
Fuel Flask   Stud   Main Engine
Starting Gear

Exploder
Mechanism   Connector Cable
and Receptacle
Depth   Assembly
Mechanism
Ballast
Water   Gyro
Compartment   Mechanism
Air Flask
**Midship
Section**

Above: A longitudinal section of the Mk 14 submarine launched torpedo.

Left: The thin white lines cutting across the sea towards the merchant ship in the foreground are the wakes of submarine torpedoes fired by the *R74* in experimental tests at Pearl Harbor, May 28, 1927.

(housing the control mechanism for guidance and the main engine and its transmission), and the tail assembly for the propellers, rudders, and elevators.

D. G. White, from an undated NAVSEA brochure, *Deckplate*.

Since Congress proved unwilling to support a vigorous postwar program of research, development, and construction of auxiliary vessels, the United States Navy was to be at a disadvantage when the Second World War began, given the fact that the other maritime powers continued to lavish money on ship construction.

After the war, R&D emphasis was on developing destroyer-launched torpedoes. The British initiated the development of a new cruiser/destroyer-launched torpedo using oxygen; and the Japanese initiated the development of a large (24-inch-diameter) destroyer-launched torpedo that ultimately evolved into the famous Long Lance (Type 93) torpedo, used most effectively during the Second World War.

During the austere postwar years, the U.S. concentrated on developing destroyer-launched torpedoes. In the early 1920s, the Naval Gun Factory in Washington, DC, and the Torpedo Station jointly developed the new 271-inch-long, three-speed (27, 34, and 46 knots) Mk 11 torpedo for use by destroyers and light cruisers. The Mk 12 destroyer-launched torpedo incorporated numerous subsystems and structural improvements that reduced the damage done to torpedoes during high-speed launches.

The Torpedo Station reflected the slowdown in Naval spending. Torpedo construction declined, and by 1923, civilian employment on Goat Island was reduced to 927. Yet despite severely constrained resources, the Station developed a variety of common torpedo components, including exploder, propulsion, and control systems to reduce cost and facilitate production and training. With the introduction of the Navy's first torpedo planes in the 1920s, the Station turned to developing air-launched weapons. Initially the first of this class of weapon was an existing torpedo simply modified for dropping from an aircraft.

Torpedo production funds for research were limited. Major emphasis was therefore on modernization of the in-service torpedoes, methods for aerial launching, and development of a new three-speed torpedo for submarines and destroyers. The Mk 11 design, which went into limited production in 1927, was the first torpedo developed entirely by the Navy. During the lean years that followed the Wall Street stock market crash of 1929, the Station worked on warheads and exploders, and on the resolution of launching problems from cruisers and destroyers traveling at maximum speed. Between 1931 and 1941 the torpedoes Mk 13, for aircraft delivery; Mk 14, for submarine launch; and Mk 15 for destroyer shots were undergoing gradual development and modification.

When the Torpedo Station production facilities completed orders for Mk 9 and Mk 10 torpedoes, the only new models produced in the United States were the new Mk 8 Mod 6 torpedoes. These units were beefed-up variants of the basic Mk 8 torpedo, strengthened to withstand the stress in high-speed launchings from cruisers. In 1923, an open-ocean range was established in Newport, with the cruiser U.S.S. *Williamson* assigned to the Station for testing exercises with the new Mk 8 Mod 6 torpedo. Conducting extensive

Clemson class destroyer DD-283 U.S.S. *Breck* transits Culebra Cut in the Panama Canal Zone on February 7, 1926. She was one of the U.S.N. vessels assigned to torpedo tests.

According to a newspaper report dated November 8, 1929, James M. Corrigan, a 75-year-old inventor was preparing to launch his radio controlled torpedo on the Jersey shore of New York Harbor. Corrigan claimed that his torpedo was larger and more destructive than any other form of torpedo; it could carry one ton of TNT at a speed of nearly 40 mph. His torpedo was 28 feet long and 3 feet in diameter. According to the inventor it could be dropped into the water from a ship or from shore, it could be made to chase its target by means of a spark set [*sic*]. The torpedo could be exploded by means of a percussion pin and a chemical fuse.

tests during the summer of 1923, and over the next several years, a number of other ships, including the U.S.S. *Breck* and the U.S.S. *Putnam*, came to the Station to conduct high-speed torpedo firings on the outside range under adverse conditions. The torpedoes damaged during these firings were studied, and the information used to strengthen and improve their ability to withstand the rigors of high-speed cruiser launchings.

By 1927, improvements to the new Mk 11 torpedo were completed, and BuOrd authorized production of the first new torpedo since the First World War. The Mk 11 had some significant performance improvements such as three speeds: 26, 34, and 46 knots, a 500-pound warhead, and a range of 15,000 yards at 26 knots.

The Mk 11, the Navy's first multi-speed model torpedo, provided the fleet with a significant increase in torpedo capabilities. Further development of an improved multi-speed torpedo to address fleet concerns resulted in the Mk 12. This torpedo was the first ever developed solely by the Naval Torpedo Station. The shell and tail assemblies were strengthened to withstand water-entry shocks, and the high-speed setting was decreased from 46 to 44 knots to reduce turbine and gear train wear. In 1928, the Navy authorized the Torpedo Station to manufacture 200 units of this improved version of the multi-speed torpedo.

Aircraft Torpedoes—The Mk 13 Torpedo

During the First World War, the British and Germans used aircraft-delivered torpedoes to attack ships. Despite the serious problem of takeoff due to the heavy weight of torpedoes attached to their undercarriages, they managed to sink ships and conclusively demonstrated that the airplane and the torpedo combined were a potent new weapon system.

The U.S. Navy closely followed these developments, and in 1920, the Navy became increasingly interested in aircraft carriers. The prime mover in the early days of naval aviation, particularly with respect to the use of the torpedo as an aircraft strike weapon, was Rear Admiral Bradley A. Fiske, U.S.N. After receiving a patent in 1912 for a torpedo-carrying airplane, Admiral Fiske proposed methods for the tactical use of aircraft torpedoes.

The Naval Air Station at Anacostia, Maryland, conducted aircraft torpedo experiments using Mk 7 Mod 5 torpedoes. A modified Curtiss biplane, with a speed of 55 knots, launched Mk 7 torpedoes at heights varying from 18 to 30 feet. Although the torpedoes launched from 30 feet experienced severe tail damage, the Navy decided that the demonstration proved the basic feasibility of a torpedo plane. As a result, BuOrd tasked the Naval Aircraft Factory in Philadelphia to design the Navy's first torpedo plane, the PT-1. The first completed PT-1 rolled out on August 30, 1921. At the same time the Station began modifying and strengthening the 18-inch, 1,700-pound Mk 7 torpedo for use on aircraft.

The establishment of an Aviation Unit at the Newport Torpedo Station in 1921 provides evidence of a growing interest in aircraft torpedo use. The Station consequently built an aircraft facility on Gould Island with a hangar and launching apron into Narragansett Bay. On November 2, 1921, Lieutenant Thomas H. Murphy, head of the Station's Air Detail, made the first successful Mk 7 torpedo drop from a PT-1 aircraft.

The Bliss-Leavitt Torpedo Mk 7 is a submarine and destroyer-launched anti-surface-ship weapon. Developed in 1911, the Mk 7 was issued to the fleet in 1912 and remained in service through the Second World War. This torpedo was also in experimentation as an aircraft launched weapon in the early 1920s.

The Navy's SC-1 twin-float torpedo bomber is test-dropping a Bliss-Leavitt Mk 7 torpedo. The Station test-dropped many Mk 7s in 1917; so impressed with the successful test drops, in 1920 the Navy commissioned its first torpedo squadron.

As the new PT-1 aircraft joined the fleet, the Navy formed its first operational aircraft torpedo plane squadron, the VY-1. On March 20, 1922, the VT-1 reported for duty on the Navy's first aircraft carrier, the *Langley*. Simultaneously, aircraft-delivered torpedoes became the heavy weapons to counter the big guns of battleships.

Throughout the 1920s, the Station conducted extensive tests with a series of new Navy torpedo planes, and the Mk 7 torpedo underwent design modifications to reduce water-entry damage and to improve it aerodynamic characteristics. By the mid-1920s as the new Douglas DT-1 torpedo plane entered the fleet, the launch envelope had been extended to accommodate plane speeds of 95 knots at 32-feet altitudes. It took skilled pilots to launch the torpedoes successfully. In spite of modifications, the delicate Mk 7 torpedo was still prone to water-entry damage and deep dives if launching conditions were not closely controlled.

These experiments proved so successful that in February 1925 the Bureau of Ordnance initiated "Project G-6" to develop a torpedo specifically for aircraft launching. The BuOrd outlined the specifications: warshot weight, 2,000 pounds; warhead charge, 350 pounds; minimum range, 4,000 yards; minimum speed, 35 knots; diameter, 21 inches; and length, not to exceed 18 feet. Specifications also instructed that the weapon was also to withstand a launching speed of 140 mph from an altitude of at least 40 feet.

Soon after its initiation, in 1926 the BuOrd discontinued the Project G-6 in favor of adapting existing 18-inch torpedoes. However, this moratorium was short-lived: on the urging of the Chief of the Bureau of Aeronautics, project G-6 was given new life in 1927. Now, the intention was to develop quickly a torpedo to meet aircraft requirements. The need was urgent: production had to begin before the existing stock of 18-inch torpedoes ran out. After a period of indecision, in 1929, specifications were again revised. The new torpedo was to have the capability to launch at 100 knots from an altitude of 50-feet. The BuOrd ordered these specifications: range, 7,000 yards; speed, minimum 30 knots; weight, 1,700 pounds; warhead charge, 400 pounds; diameter, 23 inches; length, 13 feet 6 inches.

The design evolving from these specifications in August 1930 was the 13-foot 6-inch by 22.5-inch torpedo with the designation of Mk 13. Due to the elimination of the torpedo squadron from the Carrier Air Group planned for the U.S.S. *Ranger* (CV 4), work on Project G-6 was again halted from October 1930 to July 1931.

The initial Mk 13 torpedo design incorporated many of the features from the Mk 10 Mod 2 torpedo, including its propulsion system. However, the Mk 13 development experienced numerous delays during the 1930s as BuAir and BuOrd squabbled over torpedo size, weight, and other critical requirements. Because the new torpedo planes that would be equipped with the new Mk 13s were being developed concurrently with the torpedoes, no high-performance aircraft were available to test the larger and heavier Mk 13. Consequently, it was not until the eve of the Second World War that the new Mk 13 torpedo and the new aircraft were evaluated as a total system and, as might have been predicted, serious, system-level problems needed to be resolved. In spite of all the bureaucratic disagreements, the final version of the Mk 13 torpedo met all the specifications put forward by the General Board back in 1929.

The Naval Torpedo Station on Goat Island in 1930. The view is north-west in Narragansett Bay; the small island in the middle ground is Gould Island; the large land mass above Gould is the island community of Jamestown.

The Naval Torpedo Station began the Mk 13 project in 1930. The delayed first prototypes were built in 1934. Limited research and development funding of under $100,000 per year during the lean inter-war years made it necessary to use common subsystem technologies for all three of the new torpedoes. This caused serious trouble early in the Second World War with the torpedo exploder and depth-keeping subsystems on all three torpedoes.

Mk 13 Torpedo Specifications

Length	161 inches
Diameter	22.5 inches
Weight	2,200 pounds
Speed	33.5 knots
Range	6,300 yards
Warhead	600 pounds

The Mk 13 torpedo was developed concurrently with the single-wing Douglas TBD *Devastator* torpedo bomber; however, time and money did not allow extensive evaluation. The unfortunate result was that serious problems went undiscovered until the new planes and torpedoes were used in actual combat.

By March 1933, doubts were growing as to whether there would be a torpedo plane at all. The questions arose from some undesirable features of the aircraft (T4M/TG)

Douglas TBD *Devastator*. A TBD-1 in flight, Anacostia, 1937.

April 5, 1934: view looking south showing progress of work on the new building near the yard's work piers.

January 4, 1937: progress of work on a platform for the new ferry landing.

then in use: poor performance, poor self-defense, too cumbersome, and high cost of operation and maintenance. These factors caused tactical ineffectiveness and great material losses. The Bureau of Aeronautics withdrew support for the Mk 13 type torpedo, favoring instead development of a 1,000-pound torpedo for use by bombing aircraft with these specifications: capable of launching at 125 knots from an altitude of 50-feet; range, 2,000 yards; speed, 30 knots. At this time, BuOrd considered the development of a 1,000-pound torpedo practically impossible within the current state of the art and continued with development of the Mk 13. The development was given greater importance with the outbreak of the Second World War in September 1939. Torpedo Mk 13 was available in limited members, when the United States entered the war in 1941. Aircraft employed during the war were the Douglas *Devastator* (*TBD, c.* 1937) and, later, the Grumman/General Motors *Avenger* (*TBF* and *TBM*, both *c.* 1941).

Developing the Mk 15 Destroyer Torpedo

The U.S.S. *Farragut* (DD 348) was the first destroyer built since the First World War. Commissioned in 1934, she embodied many innovations such as welded hull construction, a high-pressure steam power plant, improved gun and torpedo fire control systems, and a 5-inch 38-caliber dual-purpose gun replacing the antiquated 4-inch gun. The modern destroyer of this and later classes was equipped with multiple-mount, 21-inch torpedo tubes.

The limited inventory of Mk 11 and Mk 12 destroyer torpedoes developed and built during the economically depressed 1920s, coupled with limited warhead size of 500

U.S.S. *Farragut* (DD 348), this was the follow on 'Farragut' to the enhanced torpedo boat destroyer of 1898. She was laid down by Bethlehem Steel, Quincy, September 20 1932. Launched March 15, 1934 and commissioned June 18, 1934; decommissioned October 23, 1945.

pounds, were factors leading to the development of torpedo Mk 15 in 1931. With speed and range similar to its predecessors, the Mk 15 was longer and heavier due to the increase in the size of the warhead from 500 to 825 pounds. The Mk 15's development was completed prior to the start of the Second World War.

The Secret Exploder

In 1922 a secret project, designated G-53, was initiated to develop a new magnetic influence exploder that would increase the torpedo's effectiveness by exploding the warhead directly under the target. The exploder was activated by changes in the earth's magnetic field caused by a ship's iron hull. The design of such an exploder required a detailed knowledge of the earth's magnetic field and similar detailed knowledge of the target ships. For example, U.S. scientists learned that the magnetic signature of similar ship designs varied significantly depending on where they were built and operated (northern versus southern latitudes). During the early 1920s the Navy, with the assistance of the Carnegie Institute, conducted surveys to gather the basic information required to design an influence exploder, and an experimental magnetic influence device was ready for testing by 1926. In May of that year, a torpedo equipped with an influence exploder sank a submarine hull (ex L-8). Incredibly, this single successful test, later shown to be a fluke, provided the Navy with a basis for refusing both additional warshot tests and magnetic surveys in distant ocean areas. The extreme secrecy imposed on the project, combined with the lack of basic scientific data to support the development, hindered the development of the new influence exploder.

By 1934, a decision was made to initiate production of a new Mk 6 influence exploder for use in the Mk 14 torpedo. As a security measure, a companion Mk 5 contact exploder was developed for use in fleet issue Mk 14 torpedoes; the plan was to substitute the secret new Mk 6 influence exploder for the Mk 5 contact exploders in the event of war. Development of the Mk 6 influence exploder was so secret that the fleet was not even informed of the exploder's existence until the eve of war. Only after the Mk 6 influence exploder was actually used in combat were its serious problems revealed. Coincidentally, the Germans and the British undertook similar secret programs to develop influence exploders for their torpedoes. When employed during the Second World War, these also experienced serious deficiencies similar to those of the U.S. Navy's Mk 6.

The Electric Torpedo Mk 18—Part 1

During the First World War Germany developed an electric torpedo for use on their U-boats. At the same time, the U.S. Navy, which had first experimented with electric torpedoes in the late nineteenth century, had a secret deal with the Sperry Gyroscope Company of Brooklyn, New York, to develop a smaller version of the German weapon.

Development of the electric torpedo began with Sperry around July 1915. Prompted by the success of electric torpedoes in Germany, U.S. Navy interest continued after the Sperry contract expired. Navy in-house development of an electric torpedo continued at the Naval Experimental Station, New London, Connecticut. This design has the designation Type EL, then later Mk 1.

The electric torpedo differed from its predecessors as the battery compartment housing the energy source replaced the air flask. The engine and its accessories were replaced by an electric motor and with electrical power available electric controls were generally used. In the Mk 18, the climate of war urgency dictated the use of tried and proven pneumatic controls, with the high-pressure air stored in air bottles in the after body.

The electric torpedoes used during the Second World War utilized lead-acid secondary batteries as a power source. These required periodic maintenance—checking specific gravity of electrolyte, addition of electrolyte and periodic charging.

One of the main problems with use of submarine torpedoes was that battery maintenance was performed in the torpedo room on patrol. Alternatively, the aircraft torpedo returned to a base, carrier, or tender and could be broken down to perform the necessary battery maintenance. To facilitate maintenance, the battery compartments of submarine torpedoes were provided with hand holes, which permitted access to the batteries and provided a means of purging the compartment of hydrogen, which formed during the changing process or simply by the self-discharge of the cells while standing idle.

The Naval Torpedo Station wanted to expand the diameter of the new electric torpedo to 21-inches to increase its performance. Instead, the decision was made to build two 18-inch test vehicles because many of the major components were already on order. With limited funding, and with only one machinist working part-time on the electric torpedo project, and with only one test vehicle built, 10 range test runs were conducted. The voltage of the battery did not match the motor and the control system had problems, limiting the torpedo's speed to 18 knots. However, reports on the electric torpedo declared it wakeless, very quiet, and requiring very little service between runs.

The propulsion motor of the proposed electric torpedo was to act as a gyroscope to stabilize the torpedo in azimuth, as in the Howell torpedo. The experiment proved fruitless and all research and development was terminated in 1918 with no torpedoes ever produced.

As an economy measure, the Navy closed the New London Experimental Station in 1919. As a result, the Mk 1 project became a Torpedo Station task. Sporadic research continued over the next 25 years on the Mk 1 and Mk 2 electric torpedoes finally culminating with the Mk 20.

Because the Mk 1 electric torpedo was a low priority effort during this austere period, its funding and work force were severely limited in support of the program. During the next 5 years, 31 range runs were conducted in the Station's Narragansett Bay test range. These test runs prompted numerous modifications to the motor, propellers, control system, and battery to improve the torpedo's performance. Developing a battery capable of providing the specified speed and range was the major technical problem, causing long delays, as batteries were rebuilt or new battery designs were purchased. A disastrous range test conducted on March 31, 1928, saw the torpedo hit bottom, rupture its exercise head, break the surface, and then disappear as it traveled in an unknown direction.

Because the electric torpedo produced no wake it was impossible to locate, therefore it was considered lost. Because sufficient parts and funding were not available to assemble another electric torpedo, BuOrd directed that documentation be prepared summarizing the Mk 1 electric torpedo development and performance.

Surprisingly, in April 1930, divers working on a destroyer mooring fortuitously found the electric torpedo that had gone astray; the lost torpedo was welcomed home to the Station's shops and there it was overhauled. The Station commander requested BuOrd funding for purchasing a new battery, so that range testing could resume. Instead, BuOrd directed the Station to conduct a design study of a 21-inch-diameter electric torpedo to determine if the desired performance could be achieved in a larger vehicle with newer improved batteries.

The Station conducted a series of design studies examining the feasibility of installing an electric propulsion system in a 21-inch-diameter Mk 9 torpedo. After Station discussions with the Electric Storage Battery Company, NTS recommended to BuOrd that a Mk 9 Mod 1 torpedo be converted to electric propulsion and requested authorization to proceed. On July 21, 1931, BuOrd declared the basic feasibility of producing a reliable electric torpedo was not demonstrated and canceled the program. All research and development effort ended with the cancellation of the Mk 1 electric torpedo program.

The Onset of War in Europe

In the late 1930s, the United States placed an increased emphasis on defense, and accelerated efforts to expand torpedo production. Beginning in 1936, a series of annual facility modernization projects began on Goat Island. By 1938, Congress authorized funds for construction of new factory buildings and power plant improvements to expand the production capacity at the Torpedo Station. In July 1939, the foundation for a new "automatics" building was laid, and in October 1939, construction of a new assembly building began.

When the Second World War broke out in September 1939, the Torpedo Station's industrial facility was expanding at an unparalleled rate. Goat Island rapidly transformed from a Naval experimental activity to a major Naval industrial complex dedicated to producing ordnance. The newly constructed facilities included explosive storage units, factory buildings, an administrative building, a torpedo assembly plant, barracks, and storehouses.

Concerned about possible torpedo shortages if the United States should enter the war, Government authorized plans to further increase production. The Navy reactivated the torpedo plant at Alexandria, Virginia, expanded support facilities at Keyport, Washington, and contracted the American Can Company to build a Government-owned, contractor-operated ordnance plant in Forrest Park, Illinois.

Additional contracts were then negotiated with American Can for a second ordnance plant in St. Louis, Missouri; with the Pontiac Division of General Motors and International Harvester contracted to manufacture torpedoes in their plants. This rapid expansion placed a severe strain on the Torpedo Station, as it was the Navy's only source of torpedo manufacturing expertise available as these new production facilities came on-line.

In addition to the extensive production documentation required for the new Mks 13, 14, and 15 torpedoes just entering volume production and undertaking major expansion of the Goat Island industrial complex, the Torpedo Station had to function as the Navy's corporate memory in torpedo matters, and provide extensive support to the new production facilities. The Station provided production drawings for the various procedures and explained how to inspect and test new torpedoes.

The early torpedoes were hand-made in small job lot quantities by skilled artisans. The concept of mass production introduced a host of new problems that took years to resolve. Throughout this time, the Naval Torpedo Station grew dramatically as thousands of new employees were hired to build torpedoes. More than 2,000 people worked on Goat Island during the mid-1930s. By the early 1940s, personnel numbers had climbed to more than 12,000. While the Goat Island facilities expanded, more major building was underway at the Station's Coddington Cove and Gould Island annexes.

In this 1940 photograph the view is to the east. Jutting out on the right is the City of Newport's Long Wharf; above Long Wharf are Coaster's Harbor Island and the buildings of the Naval War Collage.

By 1940, Goat Island had become the Navy's principle torpedo design, engineering, test, and production facility. The cottages on the south end of the island are the officer's residences. To the east is the historic compact Newport waterfront.

Above: The potato farm at Coddington Cove is the site of the Torpedo Station Annex. *Official U.S.N. photograph, 1937*

Below: The Naval Underwater Ordnance Station at Coddington Cove is taking shape in early 1940s. The Still Water Basin for small observation boats, diver support craft, and torpedo retriever vessels is being built; Gould Island in the upper right.

15

The Second World War

During the early 1930s, the Torpedo Station developed the Mk 15 torpedo; by the mid-1930s, experimental production units were undergoing fleet evaluation. In this period, the *Vinson* shipbuilding program got underway, and the Navy initiated the development of new destroyers to replace the First World War vintage destroyers. Construction began on several new destroyer types (*Porter, Somer, Mahan, Benson, Sims*, and others) and evaluated various types and combinations of torpedo launcher systems: triple, quadruple, and quintuple-torpedo tube mounts.

On the eve of the Second World War, the U.S. Navy selected the new flush-decked *Fletcher*-class (DD 445) destroyer for volume production. The *Fletcher*-class destroyers and the follow-on *Sumner* and *Gearing* classes were equipped with two centerline-mounted quintuple-tube nests and were thus capable of launching 10 torpedoes in a double salvo. *Fletcher*-class destroyers built during the early part of the war, together with the *Sumner* and *Gearing* classes, provided the backbone of the Navy's destroyer force during the war. When the war started, a crash program commenced to build a class of smaller destroyer escorts (DE). Armed with one triple-barrel mount, these vessels were capable of firing a salvo of three Mk 15 torpedoes.

Mk 15 Torpedo Characteristics

Length	288 inches
Diameter	21 inches
Weight	3,841 pounds
Propulsion	Turbine
Guidance	Gyro controlled
Warhead	825 pounds of HBX
Exploder	Contact
Speed (kts)	Range (yds)
Low 26.5	15,000
Medium 33.5	10,000
High 45.0	6,000

U.S.S. *Cassin Young* (DD 793) underway in 1958. *Cassin Young* is a Fletcher Class destroyer name after Captain Cassin Young (1894–1942), who was awarded the Medal of Honor for his heroism at the Japanese attack on Pearl Harbor and who was killed in the Naval Battle of Guadalcanal in the fall of 1942. She was launched September 12, 1943 by Bethlehem Steel Corp., San Pedro, California and commissioned on December 31, 1943. She is preserved today as a memorial ship, berthed at Boston Navy Yard in Massachusetts.

The "modern" Mk 15 destroyer torpedo on deck is being prepared for loading into the torpedo magazine.

Battleship Torpedo Mk 15 is being loaded into the ship's armory. The Mk 15 was in service 1938–1956.

The Mk 15 destroyer-launched torpedo; a group of destroyer torpedo men pose with their weapon.

The multispeed Mk 12 destroyer-launched torpedo provided a state-of-the-art design base for the new torpedoes. With little research and development funding available between the wars (usually under $100,000 per year), the same subsystem technologies for the new Mks 13, 14, and 15 torpedoes had to be used. This frugality caused serious problems early in the Second World War when complications with the exploder and depth-keeping subsystems seriously limited the new torpedoes' performance.

The Mk 15 torpedo was 17 inches longer than the Mk 12 (288 inches versus 271 inches), which allowed a 300 pound increase in warhead weight. Warhead weight and size were major concerns for destroyer-launched torpedoes used primarily against heavily armored major combatants. Production began and continued during the war years to the extent that approximately 9,700 Mk 15 torpedoes were manufactured.

Above: In the waters off Montauk, New York was the closely guarded home of the U.S. Naval Torpedo Station's torpedo testing range, where newly-manufactured torpedoes were sent for final testing trials before being issued to the fleet. Here is seen an outboard shot of the torpedo Mk 15 being fired from the testing barge on the Montauk range. This is an official U.S.N. photo dated February 18, 1944.

Opposite above: In this sequence of official U.S. Navy photographs released for public information, we can appreciate the rapid progress made in building the firing pier and a variety of support structures. This April 22, 1942 photo is a view from 1,100 feet.

Opposite middle: Gould Island's north end has rapidly changed in two months, as witnessed by this June 20, 1942 photo.

Opposite below: The new firing pier and support buildings are complete and ready for operations to begin. This October 14, 1943 photo is a view from 7,000 feet.

The Second World War Torpedoes in Total

The Station had built a larger facility on Gould Island, at first for proof firing both airdropped and tube-launched weapons, and later for reworking the weapons as well. By the outbreak of the Second World War, these efforts had culminated in Navy acceptance of the torpedoes Mk 13, Mk 14, and Mk 15 as the standard weapons for aircraft, submarines, and destroyers, respectively.

In early 1942, construction began on a new firing pier at the south end of Gould Island, designed to proof-fire 100 torpedoes daily. This new facility was in service by the end of October 1942. Since the island's industrial complex was severely over-strained, a major portion of the Research, Design, and Torpedo Equipment Department moved to the new Coddington Cove Annex. In addition to the administrative and shop buildings, the new Annex had 10 torpedo storehouses and a large shipping and terminal building.

Before and during the war over 10,000 employees at the Station produced upwards of 18,000 torpedoes on site and proof-tested additional numbers manufactured at the torpedo factory in Alexandria, Virginia. All told, there were over 75,000 proofing tests on the Station's ranges during that era.

All this proof testing was not thorough enough to reveal serious design deficiencies that emerged early in the Pacific War, particularly in the Mk 14. Grave worries about torpedo performance emerged among submarine commanders early in 1942; the result of failed attacks from deep running, premature detonations, and frequent dud hits. The Navy was slow to appreciate the seriousness of the problem, preferring to blame operator error for the growing numbers of frustrated attacks. Only when submarine authorities in Pearl Harbor undertook three series of experiments—beginning in June 1942 and lasting over a year— proving that a combination of independent design faults had destabilized the torpedoes' performance did they begin to address the issue. These problems included inadequate depth control, a hypersensitive magnetic influence exploder, and deficiencies in the contact exploder mechanism. All these faults had remained undetected in the lean 1930s when a minimum of in-water tests were held. Fortunately, when the truth became known, the Navy quickly devised corrections and implemented them in both the stockpile and new production.

Even before the war, analytical alternatives to Bliss-Leavitt "steam" propulsion had emerged, at the Goat Island facility. With advances in battery technology, electric torpedoes had been feasible since the 1920s, but although several variants were built and tested, only the Mk 18 saw significant use by the U.S. Navy in the Second World War. Study began of new, higher-energy torpedo propellants because of the great increases they offered in speed and range. The most important of these were the so-called "oxygen" systems that used the decomposition of concentrated hydrogen peroxide to generate an oxidant for the primary fuel. This approach was adopted successfully by the Japanese before the war for both submarine and surface-launched torpedoes; among the latter was the infamous 24 inch "Long Lance," which emerged as the most effective destroyer torpedo of the conflict.

Each torpedo-firing pier is equipped with a Mk 24 deck tube with automatic setter, an 18 inch British deck tube, and a drop rack for testing aircraft torpedoes.

During the height of the Second World War as many as 100 torpedoes were test fired daily. In this 1944 photo a Mk 13 aircraft torpedo is leaving the tube.

The Mk 15 in the Battle of Leyte Gulf

The Battle of Leyte Gulf in the campaign to re-take the Philippines still stands as the largest sea battle ever fought. When the combined Japanese Fleet sortied to attack the American fleet, U.S. Navy destroyers and torpedo boats decimated Admiral Nishimura's Southern Task Force by torpedo attacks conducted as they crossed the Surigao Straits. Admiral Oldendorf used his destroyers and torpedo boats to ambush Nishimura's force of two battleships, a cruiser, and four destroyers, forcing them to run a Mk 15 torpedo gauntlet as they passed through the narrow straits at night. Oldendorf's battleships massed at the exit of the straits and their murderous concentrated fire forced the surviving Japanese ships to turn tail and attempt to escape by again running the torpedo gauntlet. The sole survivor of this torpedo onslaught was the *Shigure*, the same fortunate destroyer that had survived the *Moosbrugger's* torpedo attack in the Gizo Straits in August 1943.

During the same Battle, Admiral Kurita's Central Force of two battleships, nine cruisers, and eleven destroyers made a high-speed transit of the San Bernardino Straits during the night. At 0648 hours, they started shelling Rear Admiral Clinton A. Sprague's Task Group 77.4.3 (Taffy 3), consisting of six escort carriers, four destroyers, and three destroyer escorts that were providing air support for the invasion forces. Sprague launched all available aircraft to attack the Japanese ships, which left his six unarmored escort carriers unprotected, and it appeared disaster was imminent. With a two-to-one speed advantage, the Japanese rapidly closed in on the small thin-skinned carriers, and the big guns were taking their toll. To buy time, Sprague ordered his destroyers and destroyer escorts to lay smoke screens and conduct torpedo attacks against the vastly superior Japanese force.

The fleet was taking a savage mauling from the Japanese battleships, but when the U.S. ships fired torpedoes, the Japanese took evasive action. The destroyer *Johnston* made a hit on the cruiser *Kumano*, forcing it and the bomb-damaged *Suzuya* out of the battle. Although the ships and planes soon exhausted their torpedoes, simulated torpedo attacks continued against the Japanese, forcing them into constant evasive action, and preventing them from again closing in on the U.S. carriers. American planes then sank two more Japanese cruisers, and Kurita—not realizing that victory was within his grasp—broke off the engagement. This again demonstrated the lessons of Tsushima and Jutland: that an enemy battle line would not press home an attack when confronted by aggressive destroyer torpedo fire.

Although the Mk 15 torpedo did not match the performance of Japan's larger, destroyer-launched Long Lance torpedo, once the Mk 15's exploder and depth-keeping problems were solved it proved a reliable and effective weapon. In terms of ships sunk, the Mk 15 torpedo made a substantial contribution in the Pacific campaign; its performance provided a fitting final demonstration of the effectiveness of destroyer-launched torpedoes.

The Naval Torpedo Station and the Naval Ordnance Plant in Forest Park, Illinois, were the principal manufacturing sites for the Mk 15 torpedo. Nearly 11,000 Mk 15s were produced in four Mods (0, 1, 2, and 3) during the war, and some 7,800 of these were issued to the fleet.

The Electric Torpedo Mk 18—Part 2

During the interwar years the Germans had continued secretly developing their electric torpedo. During the Second World War, the improved German G7e electric torpedo proved its worth by sinking millions of tons of allied shipping.

Capture of the intact German submarine U-570 in 1941 gave the U.S. Navy a German G7e electric torpedo in January 1942, which led to the development of torpedo Mk 18 by Westinghouse Electric Company at its Sharon, PA facility. Within 15 weeks, the first prototype was delivered to the Station for evaluation. Six months from the date of contract award, the first six production units were delivered. Torpedo Mk 18 is credited with having sent to the bottom one million tons of Japanese shipping during the Second World War. In addition to being wakeless, electric torpedoes such as the Mk 18 required only about 70 percent of the labor required to manufacture a torpedo with thermal propulsion.

The Growth of the Station during the War

Along with the massive increase in its workforce, Station funding for production and research at the NTS grew from $63,000 in 1931 to $7.5 million in 1940, and soared to $47 million in 1943. By March 1944, Station employment had reached a record 12,995 civilians and 1,127 military personnel.

Problems at Midway

In 1942, during the Battle of Midway, *TBD* bomber squadrons became separated from their fighter escorts and had to attack Japanese carriers without fighter protection. Because the torpedo bombers posed a major threat to the carriers, the enemy sent all available fighters to attack the slow, unescorted bombers. The nimble Japanese *Zero* fighters had a turkey shoot. Thirty-five of the 41 *TBDs* were shot down without scoring a single torpedo hit. However, while the Zeros were being refueled and rearmed, U.S. dive-bombers and fighters arrived. The unopposed U.S. planes attacked aggressively. Although the sacrifice of the *TBDs* was not a planned tactic, it was a major factor in the U.S. Navy's victory at Midway.

Mk 13 Improvements

Midway demonstrated that successful Mk 13 airdrops required slow, low-altitude, high-risk flying under fighter escort. An urgent effort was started to make weapon performance match the higher performance of the Grumman *TBF* torpedo bomber that entered the fleet in 1942. This involved two projects, a crash program to improve the Mk 13, and development of a new aircraft torpedo, the Mk 25.

The first production TBF-1 *Avenger* performed its initial flight on December 30, 1941, with formal Navy acceptance following on January 30. A total of 1,123 TBF-1s would be built in all. The Avenger was Grumman's first torpedo bomber. It was a barrel-shaped, low-wing aircraft that a clear resemblance to a scaled-up Grumman F4F Wildcat fighter.

The Navy's hard-hitting Grumman/General Motors *Avenger* carrier-based torpedo bomber; this fighter-bomber carries a payload of three Mk 13 torpedoes.

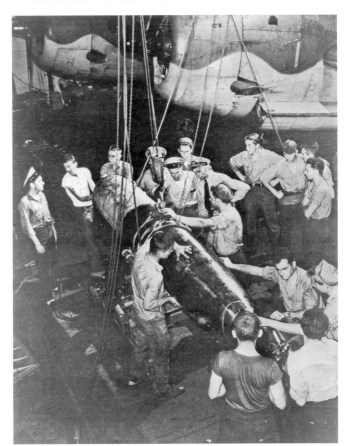

In this official Navy photograph dated October 23, 1942, a crew at the Guadalcanal Airport in the Pacific campaign is loading a Mk 13 torpedo onto the carriage of an *Avenger* torpedo bomber.

Experts in aerodynamics and hydrodynamics from the California Institute of Technology began working with the Navy. To help in evaluating torpedo airdrops; high-speed strip cameras were installed at the Naval Torpedo Station range in Narragansett Bay. All told, more than 4,300 experimental torpedo launchings were conducted and analyzed. Improvements were incorporated to extend the Mk 13 torpedo's launch parameters. The improvements ranged from minor modifications on igniters, to the addition of a stabilizing shroud ring.

Because of this crash program, the Mk 13's deadliness improved dramatically. Now, it could be launched at aircraft speeds up to 410 knots and from an altitude of 2,400 feet, versus 110 knots and 50 feet previously. Ultimately, the Mk 13 proved to be a highly reliable and effective weapon. Additionally, as production caught up with wartime needs, the Mk 13 replaced the Mk 8 as the standard patrol-torpedo boat torpedo, launched from deck-mounted roll-off racks. Starting with the Mk 13 Mod 0 and ending with the Mk 13 Mod 13, some 17,000 of these torpedoes were produced during the war by five different facilities: Naval Torpedo Station, Newport; Naval Ordnance Plants in St. Louis, MO, and Forest Park, IL; the GM Pontiac Division; and the International Harvester Company.

In this *c.* 1941 U.S.N. photo the view is of the south end of Gould Island showing the Naval Torpedo Station's floatplane runway and plane's enclosure. Gould Island is located a short distance west of Goat Island. In the background is the island community of Jamestown, Rhode Island.

The "Best" Aircraft Torpedo

By 1944, performance reports from the fleet concerning the Mk 13 reflected the intensive improvement efforts. The weapon now received high praise. During the war, Mk 13 torpedoes sank about 1,000,000 tons of enemy ships. By the end of the conflict, the Mk 13 was being called "the best aircraft torpedo in the world."

One final combat mission lay ahead for the Mk 13 torpedo. During the Korean War, repeated bombing attacks failed to damage the crucial North Korean Hwachon Dam. Then eight *Skyraiders* scored six hits with Mk 13 torpedoes and destroyed the dam. This demonstrated once more the versatility and effectiveness of the Mk 13.

In the 1950s, large-scale cutbacks in surface naval forces and the demise of the battleship reduced the need for aircraft-dropped torpedoes. A new era of undersea warfare was emerging, and smaller homing torpedoes designed to counter the growing submarine threat soon replaced the Mk 13.

> The first use in combat was successful beyond all expectations. A torpedo squadron in August 1944 launched nine torpedoes equipped with rag rings, shroud rings, and sank four Japanese cargo ships. Observers reported, no torpedoes were seen to miss.

Source: NUWC Technical Document 10,056, July 1992.

If anyone still needed to be convinced that the aircraft torpedo could pull its weight in this war, he had his answer when the Commander First Carrier Task Force made the following comment on the shroud ring torpedo: "the torpedo equipped with the Mk 1 shroud ring surpassed expectations. Almost 100% performance was experienced in all attacks. In attacks on shipping in Manila Bay, one squadron dropped 13 torpedoes in water of an average of 48 feet. All torpedoes made hot, straight, and normal runs. Seven of them were hits. Personnel responsible for the development of the Mk 1 shroud ring are to be highly commended."

Naval Aviation News, March 15, 1945.

The Mk 14 Submarine-Launched Torpedo

The submarine torpedo of 1930 consisted of torpedo Mk 7 (18-inch tubes), torpedo Mk 9 (converted from battleship torpedoes) and torpedo Mk 10 (developed about 1915). The development of the torpedo Mk 14 during the 1930s provided a 21-inch modern steam torpedo with a two-speed range capability and large warhead. By the mid-1930s, prototype production of Mk 14 torpedoes was in progress at the Newport Naval Torpedo Station; by 1938, limited numbers of Mk 14 torpedoes were being evaluated on the long-range fleet submarines (with their longer torpedo tubes), which began to enter the fleet during the 1930s. These included the *Salmon* and *Plunger* classes (mid-1930s) and the *Tambor* and *Gato* classes (late 1930s), the latter two classes having 10 torpedo tubes (6 forward and 4 aft). During the pre-war period, Mk 14 torpedoes were in short supply, and the Navy was reluctant to conduct warshot tests for fear of depleting a limited inventory. Consequently, the majority of test firings were conducted with exercise-configured Mk 14 torpedoes, and serious problems with warshot-configured Mk 14 torpedoes remained undetected until they were actually used in combat operations when the war began.

Major Torpedo Problems during the War

The Second World War was the first conflict in which the U.S. Navy expended large numbers of torpedoes, and most of the problems with torpedo performance arose from two root causes:

Subtle but critically important differences between the weight and trim of exercise and warshot torpedoes; and

A reluctance, based on a false economy, to expend warshot torpedoes in peacetime fleet exercises against real targets.

If the Second World War had been fought on the Naval Torpedo Station's Newport range using exercise torpedoes, there would have been no serious problems; however, the war was fought in the Pacific Ocean with warshot-configured torpedoes. The combination of the difference in weight and trim between warshot and exercise torpedoes (running depth errors), differences in the earth's magnetic fields (northern versus southern latitudes), and the lack of realistic warshot exploder tests (exploder not used in exercise firings) created a series of torpedo crises early in the war.

Because submarines were expending the largest number of torpedoes, they experienced the most problems. Relations between the submarine force and the ordnance suppliers deteriorated rapidly when the Mk 14 torpedo failed to match expectations. The fleet complained that the *warshot* torpedoes were faulty, but the BuOrd and Newport Naval Torpedo Station, after conducting extensive tests with *exercise* torpedoes, maintained that the torpedoes were operating properly.

When war began, the U.S. Navy finally confirmed in combat that its First World War vintage warshot torpedoes were, along with both German and British torpedoes, running deep. The problem was easily solved by providing new depth calibrations for warshot-configured torpedoes, but this problem provided a strong indication that the lack of realistic fleet testing and evaluation of warshot torpedoes in peacetime was a serious error that would haunt the Navy in wartime.

Exploders Perform Erratically

When the new Mk 13, Mk 14, and Mk 15 torpedoes were used in combat, complaints about warshot failures poured into BuOrd from operational commanders. Controlled tests in which warshot-trimmed torpedoes were fired at nets to accurately check their operating depth against the preset depth were conducted on the Naval Torpedo Station's range; it was confirmed that the new torpedoes, like their First World War counterparts, also ran deeper with the heavier warheads installed. The fleet was provided with data to correct the depth error, but the submarine force continued to complain about the poor performance of the Mk 14 torpedo.

The new secret Mk 6 influence exploder came under suspicion due to frequent reports that Mk 14 torpedoes equipped with the exploder were detonating prematurely when 50 feet short of the target. Much ill will was generated as the operational forces and the technical services traded angry accusations concerning the poor performance of the Mk 14. During this turbulent period, Admiral Lockwood directed Pacific Fleet Submarines (SUBPAC) to deactivate the Mk 6 influence exploder and use the contact exploder for all firings, while Admiral Christie, who had worked on the Mk 6 exploder, ordered Southwest Pacific Submarines to continue using the Mk 6 influence exploder.

As the exploder's erratic performance in the South Pacific was confirmed by evidence, the Mk 6 was taken out of service, and a crash program initiated to correct its problems and develop a new influence exploder. The Torpedo Station quickly conducted a program to dramatically enhance the Mk 6 exploder's performance; at the same time as a new backup influence exploder (Mk 10) was developed. However, the submarine force, disenchanted with the poor performance of the Mk 6, lost all interest in influence exploders and continued to use contact exploders for the rest of the war.

With discontinued use of the influence exploder, fleet complaints about "dud shots" using the contact exploder increased markedly. In responding, BuOrd and the Torpedo Station suggested that part of the problem might be due to imperfectly trained submarine crews claiming dud shots when they actually failed to be on target. This response generated a new round of bitter exchanges between the fleet and BuOrd. The validity of the fleet complaints was dramatically demonstrated on July 24, 1943 when torpedoes fired by the submarine U.S.S. *Tinosa* (SS 283) disabled a large Japanese whaling factory ship. The *Tinosa* closed to sure-shot range to finish off the ship and proceeded to fire dud after dud at the stationary target. During this attack, 15 torpedoes were fired and 12 hits were claimed. The *Tinosa* saved its last torpedo and brought it back to Pearl Harbor for examination. Less than a month later, U.S.S. *Haddock* (SS 231) disabled a 10,000-ton Japanese tanker and proceeded to fire 11 more torpedoes at the damaged ship without getting a single warhead explosion.

This confirmed poor performance finally got the attention of SUBPAC, BuOrd and the Newport Torpedo Station, and extensive testing was initiated in Chesapeake Bay, Pearl Harbor, and Narragansett Bay. These tests revealed that the contact exploder worked well for glancing or angle hits, but when the torpedo hit the target broadside (at a right angle to the target) at 45 knots, the impact bent the firing pin and the exploder failed to function. Tests conducted both at Pearl Harbor and Newport confirmed that the firing pin was the culprit. To solve the problem, SUBPAC proposed a lighter firing pin, while the Torpedo Station proposed a heavier spring for the firing pin. BuOrd, not wanting to take any chances, opted for a "belt and suspenders" solution by incorporating both a lighter firing pin and heavier spring to be sure that the problem was solved.

It took almost one-and-a-half years of frantic effort to correct warshot problems that could have been identified before the war if realistic warshot torpedo firing exercises had been conducted in peacetime. From mid-1943, with the warshot problems corrected, the Mk 14 showed itself to be a highly reliable and effective weapon. Ultimately, when the post-war statistics were compiled, the Mk 14 proved to be a most exceptional torpedo: it had sunk over 4 million tons of Japanese shipping. Only the Germans' G-series (G-7-a and G-7-e) torpedoes had put more tonnage on the ocean bed.

With Mk 14 production beginning by the Second World War, approximately 13,000 torpedoes of this type were manufactured during the war years. The mainstay of the submarine force in the war until the introduction of the wakeless, electric torpedo Mk 18 in 1944, the Mk 14 is credited with sinking roughly 4,000,000 tons of Japanese shipping.

Originally designed and produced for mechanical fire control settings, torpedo Mk 14 was modified to be compatible with modern electrical-set fire control systems, and continues in service in today's submarine forces.

Wartime demands for more torpedoes and scarcity of materials in 1943 led to the development and manufacture of torpedo Mk 23, a short-range, high-speed torpedo 4,500 yards at 46 knots). Identical to the Mk 14 without the low-speed feature, this torpedo was not favored by the fighting forces, since the multispeed option of the Mk 14 permitted greater tactical flexibility, especially during the latter stages of the war, when escorts that were more sophisticated and ASW tactics forced firing from longer ranges.

Mk 14 Torpedo Characteristics

Length	246 inches
Diameter	21 inches
Weight	3,282 pounds
Propulsion	Turbine
Guidance	Gyro
Warhead	643 lb of HBX

Speed (knots)		Range (yards)
Low	31.1	9,000
High	46.3	4,500

Mk 14 Torpedo's Role in Achieving Victory

The 50,000-man submarine force represented less than two percent of the U.S. Navy's wartime complement; yet fleet submarines, employing Mk 14 torpedoes as their principal weapon, accounted for 55 percent of Japan's maritime losses. These submarines devastated the Japanese merchant fleet, sinking more than 5 million tons of shipping. By 1945, the Japanese were so short of oil that even their most high-priority combat operations were curtailed.

Although severing Japan's sea-lanes of supply and communication was the submarine force's primary mission, SUBPAC submarines (and their Mk 14 torpedoes) also played a major role in the naval war, accounting for almost one third of all Japanese warships destroyed during the war. SUBPAC submarines frequently went head to head with Japanese destroyers and escorts during convoy attacks and outfought them by a six-to-one ratio (six escorts sunk by submarines for every submarine sunk by an escort).

There is no denying that the serious operational problems encountered early in the war placed the Mk 14 torpedo high on the Navy's problem list. Many naval historians discuss the Mk 14 torpedo "scandal" in detail, citing it as a classic example of the poor quality of the weapons provided to the fleet, and the problems between the fleet and the producers. These problems were real and it is entirely appropriate that they be addressed. It is unfortunate, however, that these writers, when discussing Mk 14 warshot torpedo problems, fail to document its impressive wartime accomplishments. The final evaluation of a weapon is its demonstrated performance in combat. The Mk 14 torpedo's world-class record for performance has been largely ignored. It is ironic that the Mk 14, which entered the Second World War as a problem-plagued and unreliable weapon, ended up as the single most destructive weapon employed by the U.S. Navy during the war. It accounted for about 80 percent of Japan's merchant ship losses and about 20 percent of Japan's naval losses. This massive destruction, accomplished with a wartime expenditure of fewer than 5,000 torpedoes, attests to the overall effectiveness of the Mk 14; clearly, it was a first-rate weapon.

Four Decades of Service

The Mk 14 torpedo was the last of the U.S. Navy's artisan-built torpedoes that were direct descendants of, and closely resembled, the early Whitehead designs. Its life cycle, from initial development in the early 1930s until its retirement in 1980, spanned almost half a century, and it was the Navy's principal anti-ship torpedo for more than four decades. During the Mk 14's later life, the submarine force developed a sentimental attachment to it. Even the skippers of nuclear-powered, ballistic missile submarines, with their massive destructive potential, enjoyed conducting Mk 14 torpedo firings. The Mk 14 was the last link with the Second World War submarine era, a time when submarine warfare involved making an undetected approach, getting a target ship in the periscope cross hairs, and watching the torpedo's wake intersect the target. The last of the gyro-guided, straight-running torpedoes, the Mk 14 dramatically demonstrated the destructive potential of guided weapons. However, the Mk 14 was overtaken by new technology as homing torpedoes replaced guided ones. When the wire-guided Mk 48 Mot 1 torpedo, with its active/passive homing system, began entering the fleet in the early 1970s, the Mk 14 Mod 5 torpedoes were removed. By 1980, all operational submarines were Mk 48 equipped, and the Mk 14 torpedo, with more than four decades of active service, was "retired with honors."

The Passive Acoustic Homing Torpedo

In 1943, it was learned that the Germans were using a torpedo, affectionately called the "GNAT," the German Naval Acoustic Torpedo with terminal homing—a torpedo that guided itself to the target by the noise generated by the ship's propellers (cavitation). Prior knowledge of Germany's development of the GNAT had already leaked to U.S. Intelligence some time before, and in 1940, the National Defense Research Committee Office of Scientific Research and Development sponsored a project to develop an acoustic homing torpedo. Western Electric headed the project; central to the homing system effort was the Bell Telephone Laboratories and the Harvard Underwater Sound laboratory.

Engineering development of the torpedo, mine Mk 24 (for security reasons it was known by the code name "Fido"), was assigned to Western Electric Company, Kearney, NJ, and at the General Electric Company, Erie Works, and later at the General Electric Company, Philadelphia, PA. Approximately 100,000 units were ordered, but the order was reduced due to the high effectiveness of the weapon.

The Brush Development Company, Cleveland, Ohio, concurrent with the so-called mine Mk 30 developed the mine Mk 24 because of apprehension regarding the acoustic steering ability of the Mk 24. Simply to deceive enemy spies, the Mk 24 torpedo was called a mine. The torpedo Mk 24 was developed as an outgrowth of work on an underwater listening device sponsored by the Naval Defense Research Committee during the Second World War.

This torpedo, with a small warhead, was a crippling weapon designed for "mission kill" vice "platform kill." Approximately 4,000 of these aircraft-launched, passive acoustic, anti-submarine torpedoes were produced and in service during the War and subsequent years until replaced by torpedo Mk 34.

The mine Mk 30 was unique in that it was only 10 inches in diameter and weighed only 265 pounds including a 50-pound warhead. It was nearly identical to torpedo Mk 43 Mod 1, which was to follow a decade later except that the mine Mk 30 employed passive acoustic bearing system rather than the active acoustic homing system of the torpedo Mk 43 Mod 1.

The Second World War
National Defense Research Committee (1939–1950)

Early in the Second World War, in June 1940, President F. D. Roosevelt appointed eminent civilian scientists to the National Defense Research Committee. Harvard University President Dr. James B. Conat became chairman. Others named were Dr. Karl Compton, President of the Massachusetts Institute of Technology, and Dr. Frank B. Jewett, President of the National Academy of Science. The Committee was established as a unit of the Office of Scientific Research and Development (OSRD), and was headed by Dr. Vannever Bush, President of the Carnegie Institution in Washington, DC. The chief objectives of the Committee were to recommend to the OSRD suitable projects and research programs on the instruments of war, and initiate research projects on the request of the U.S. Army and Navy or allied counterparts. The committee consisted of 23 divisions, each specializing in particular field.

Division 6, concerned with sub-surface warfare, and headed by Dr. John T. Tate was the group tasked with the torpedo research and development role. The division's first objective was:

> … the most complete investigation possible of all the factors and phenomena involved in the accurate detection of submerged or partially submerged submarines and in anti-submarine devices.

Through the systematic study of all phases of underwater acoustics, the groundwork was laid permitting engineering development and deployment of the acoustic homing torpedo during the Second World War.

Summary

Torpedo production during the Second World War years 1941–1945, totaled about 17,000. The peak was 5,656 torpedoes in 1944. During this five-year period, 7,500 torpedoes were proof-fired on the Gould Island range. The Mk 14 Mod 3A was the most widely used torpedo in the war, accounting for four million tons of Japanese shipping. The Mk 13 aircraft torpedo also played an important role in the war in the Pacific. Lack of familiarity and the requirement for a low altitude, low speed launch discouraged its use by Navy aviators early in the war. Extensive Torpedo Station test programs that test dropped 4,300 torpedoes, and the development of a stabilizer, drag ring, and shroud ring restored confidence in the Mk 13. These permitted an increase in launching speed from 110 knots to 410 knots, and in altitude from 50 feet to 2,400 feet.

Some major production problems had to be overcome. Since large manufacturers had little interest in the torpedo program, the Torpedo Station at Newport was obliged to do business with 200 small piece part contractors. Training unskilled labor and a high annual turnover among Station personnel were continuing difficulties. Despite these problems, the Station was awarded the Navy "E" for excellence in production of naval ordnance six times during the war years.

The Naval Torpedo Station discontinued the manufacture of torpedoes in 1945. The primary reason was the end of the war with its attendant cutback in torpedo needs. The Station's post-war mission, as outlined by the Bureau of Ordnance, included design, research, and experimental torpedo work; ranging and proofing of torpedoes; and storage and issue of torpedoes and component parts.

The Station discontinued the manufacture of torpedoes in 1945. However, some engineering work continued. The hustle and bustle of workers during the years of high-volume production had ended. Except for a few training and yard work craft, the torpedo boat wharfs are empty. In the lower left of the photo is the employee's shuttle ferry and ferry slip.

16

The Continuing Mission

Post Second World War

The years following the Second World War brought sweeping organizational and program changes to the Naval Torpedo Station. With a new name and mission, the migration of all Navy facilities from Goat Island was completed and the island returned to civilian ownership. Only two miles north on Narragansett Bay to Coddington Cove, the Station settled on several acres of farmland where it remains today. From the production-oriented role imposed by the war to meet the demands of rapidly expanding technology, the Torpedo Station broadened and synthesized its program responsibilities. The generic beginnings of much of the work currently at the Naval Undersea Warfare Center are direct results of extraordinarily successful programs developed during this period by the Center's predecessors—the Naval Underwater Ordnance Station (NUOS) and the Naval Underwater Weapons Systems Engineering Center (NAVUWSEC), formally the Central Torpedo Office.

NUOS

In December 1951, establishment of the Naval Underwater Ordnance Station, a research and development laboratory replaced the Torpedo Station. During its existence, NUOS made dramatic progress in areas such as propulsion, range instrumentation, fire control systems, launchers, explosive echo ranging, and oceanography. NUOS originated the idea for the weapons range at the Atlantic Undersea Test and Evaluation Center (AUTEC) and subsequently followed through as a lead activity in the planning and establishment of this over $100 million technical evaluation facility in the Bahamas.

At the time of the merger with NAVUWSEC, civilian employees numbered 750, one-third of who were engineers and scientists, one-third skilled artisans, and one-third semi-professional and administrative personnel. Additionally, about 100 military people were assigned to NUOS.

It was not long before NUOS assumed a key role in the development of the wire-guided, electrically driven acoustic homing torpedo, the Mk 37, which reached the Fleet in 1956. It then embarked on a technology program to prepare the ground for a

Above: As seen in this official U.S. Navy photograph dated June 19, 1973, the Still Water Basin is operational and the breakwater is complete.

Below: Interior of the torpedo test-firing facility after declared surplus property and abandoned by the Navy sometime in the mid-1960s.

new generation of heavyweight submarine torpedoes responsive to the growing Soviet threat. New high-energy-density propulsion systems and sophisticated acoustic homing technologies were explored, and Newport Laboratory later collaborated with Clevite-Gould and Westinghouse on the engineering development and Fleet introduction of the resulting Torpedo Mk 48 in the early 1970s. Later, they also managed the development of the Mk 48 Advanced Capability (ADCAP) torpedo that appeared subsequently in 1989. Both of these use Otto fuel, a chemical monopropellant that contains its own oxidizer.

NAVUWSEC

Established in 1941 as the Central Torpedo Office (CTO) under the Torpedo Station, the primary duties of NAVUWSEC were to coordinate and expedite production for private and other government manufacturers. In 1947, with broadened technical responsibilities, CTO became an independent naval activity. Assignment of still broader mission responsibilities in mid-1963 brought a major reorganization and the name Naval Underwater Weapons Systems Engineering Center. From comparatively meager personnel and mission beginnings, NAVUWSEC at the time of the merger with NUOS had grown to an employment level of about 500 civilians and its mission had expanded to include in-service engineering and technical responsibilities for procurement, production, maintenance, quality assurance and evaluation and Fleet readiness. Much pioneer work for present NUWC programs in these areas was accomplished by NAVUWSAC.

NUWS

NUOS and NAVUWSEC merged in 1966 to form Naval Underwater Weapons Station (NUWS). The merger implemented Department of Defense management policy to place "conception to grave" responsibility with one activity. Accordingly, NUOS with its extensive undersea research and development capabilities and NAVUWSEC's knowledge of undersea production and service engineering, quality assurance and evaluation and maintenance were brought under "one roof."

NUWRES

In the aftermath of realigning Navy Research and Development center responsibilities in the early 1990s, the Newport complex—by now renamed the Naval Underwater Weapons Research and Engineering Station (NUWRES)—inherited technical responsibility for air-dropped and surface-launched lightweight torpedoes from the former Naval Ocean Systems Center in San Diego, California. These included the battery-powered Torpedo Mk 44, first introduced in 1956, and its widely deployed successor, the Torpedo Mk 46, which

As seen in this July 11, 1973 photo, the Gould Island test-firing facility is almost totally abandoned. All of the sundry support structures are gone and a large portion of the island has been reclaimed by nature. Since the mid-1990s the firing pier has become a crumbling mass of brick and cement; the island is overgrown with brambles and conifers; it is home to a small deer population and a variety of animals and migratory birds.

first appeared in 1963 using solid chemical fuel, but was then modified in 1967 to employ liquid monopropellant. Subsequently, the facility collaborated with Honeywell/Alliant Tech in developing the Torpedo Mk 50—formerly the Advanced Lightweight Torpedo—that was fielded in limited numbers in 1994 employing a Stored Chemical Energy Propulsion System (SCEPS) based on a lithium-fluorine reaction to achieve high speed and deep diving capability. The best of both Mk 48 ADCAP and Mk 50 technology was combined to develop a new and affordable Mk 54 Lightweight Hybrid Torpedo optimized for shallow-water operations.

NUSC and NUWC

The Naval Underwater Systems Center was formed in 1970 by the merger of two independent laboratories of the Naval Material Command: the Naval Underwater Weapons Research and Engineering Station, Newport, Rhode Island, and the Navy

Underwater Sound Laboratory, New London, Connecticut. These two complexes formed the principal laboratories of NUSC. In July 1971, the Atlantic Undersea Test and Evaluation Center (AUTEC) in the Bahamas was made a detachment of NUSC.

The joining of these navy laboratories formed the Naval Underwater Systems Center (NUSC), with broad responsibilities across the entire spectrum of undersea warfare. Finally, in 1992, the Systems Center teamed with the Naval Underwater Weapons Engineering Station, Keyport, Washington to form today's Naval Undersea Warfare Center (NUWC), with headquarters in Newport. Today, the Center is active in research, development, and in-service engineering for torpedoes and other tactical submarine-launched weapons: Anti-submarine Warfare (ASW) mobile targets, countermeasures, unmanned underwater vehicles (UUVs), sonar, underwater fire control, and a wide range of submarine auxiliary components, such as periscopes and antennas.

Work at Newport has focused on research and development in such diverse areas as torpedo propulsion, range instrumentation, fire control systems, launches, explosives, echo ranging, and oceanography. In service, engineering has provided the Navy with expertise for procurement, production, maintenance, and quality assurance.

The now closed New London Laboratory descended from two Second World War laboratories operated by the National Defense Research Committee: The Columbia University Division of War Research and the Harvard Underwater Sound Laboratory. The Columbia Laboratory at New London worked chiefly on the development of passive sonar devices, while the Harvard Laboratory at Cambridge investigated echo-ranging sonar and originated early scanning sonar techniques. In 1945, the sonar portion of the Harvard Laboratory transferred to New London and merged with the work of the Columbia Laboratory, creating the Naval Underwater Sound Laboratory.

A basic and applied research program supporting systems development is a major thrust at the Center, and activities at NUSC cover all phases of the Center's primary mission responsibilities for programs in surface ship and submarine sonar, anti-submarine warfare weapons, combat control, launches, and undersea ranges, including management of the AUTEC range complex.

Today, Goat Island, offshore of fashionable downtown Newport, is the site of a modern luxury hotel, high-end condominiums, and a marina. Only a fragment remains to excite memories of the once bustling industrial complex.

Major Scientific and Technical Facilities

The Submarine Sonar Department conducts research, development, and engineering directed toward all acoustic elements of submarine combat systems. Areas of responsibility include active and passive detection, classification, tracking and localization, acoustic communications, and acoustic warfare. The department also provides system employment guidelines and operational training systems, and supports center wide acoustic transduction requirements.

Above: This 1994 photograph reveals the complex Naval Undersea Warfare Center, Newport Division where advanced underwater science and technology are explored.

Below left: Naval Undersea Warfare Center technicians are lowering a Mk 30 anti-submarine mobile target into the Center's acoustic test tank.

Below right: Naval Undersea Warfare Center engineers and technicians prepare a Submarine Tactical Array Sonar System for testing and evaluation at the Center's complex at the Dodge Pond facility at East Lyme, Connecticut.

The Transient Processing Laboratory is used to develop and evaluate real-time, multibeam transient detection and classifications algorithms. The Laboratory includes a mobile, multi-beam testbed for evaluating algorithms in the laboratory and at sea, and a general-purpose system for developing and analyzing algorithms and support software.

The Passive Signal Processing Laboratory supports advanced techniques for signal processing of towed array acoustic information for Towed Array Sonar Technology (TAST) programs are developed in this laboratory. Systolic array, very large scale integration (VLSI) technology is being applied to towed array beam forming requirements. As many as four individual host computer configurations with associated input and output equipment form the essential research tools for the TAST program.

The Classified Signal Processing Facility is an approved facility used to process classified acoustic data. It provides data analysis in support of various Navy R&D programs, including the Transient Acoustic Processor, the Mk 48 torpedo, and the TOMAHAWK cruise missile. It has also been used for Arctic research and system damage assessment.

Advanced Conformal Submarine Acoustic Sensor Laboratory's primary purpose is data analysis for the ACSAS experiments with the Kamloops vehicle. Kamloops experiments are designed to evaluate new methods of flow noise reduction and characterize direct flow noise as a function of frequency, vehicle speed, and array dimensions. The software used to perform this data analysis was developed at the facility. Other uses of the facility are developing software models to investigate beam forming techniques and weighting schemes for large non-planar arrays.

The Low Ship Impact Ranging Facility term refers to a target ranging methodology that may be implemented in the Fleet without a major physical impact on ships or their sonar. The key element of this facility is a Multipath Range and Depth Estimator, which is an engineering breadboard assembly of commercial array processors, computers, and displays. MRADE processes acoustic signals from a host sonar, detects differences in arrival times due to differences in propagation paths, and uses these differences to determine the range and depth of the signal source.

Wide Aperture Array Facility develops hardware and software for the support of the submarine Wide Aperture Array sonar system. Its primary purpose is to integrate various computers and test instrumentation into a coherent and unified data acquisition suite. Portions of the system become a portable laboratory for installation in the test submarine during at-sea tests of the WAA sonar system.

High & Medium Frequency Active Sonar Computer Laboratory was originally configured to develop and test advanced development model software for active detection systems such as Submarine Active Detection Sonar and Mine Detection and Avoidance Sonar. The facility is now used to analyze sea test data to explore processing options for single and multi-ping processing algorithms. It also supports computer-aided classification investigations involving clue evaluation and cluster reduction.

Advanced Sonar Development Facility is an acoustic test bed where submarine combat systems algorithms for detection, classification, tracking, and contact correlation are integrated and evaluated. It is used in support of various submarine tasks, including Submarine Advanced Combat Systems (SUBACS) advanced development, AN/BQQ-5 sonar improvement, and Wide Aperture Array software development and data analysis. It includes VAX-11/780 and 11/730 computers, two Ramtek displays, and array processor, a signal processor, disk and tape storage devices, plotter, printers, and terminals.

The Acoustic Communications Laboratory serves a dual purpose. First, because NUSC is responsible for all installations/removals of AN/WQC-6 acoustic communications equipment on the East Coast, it serves as a staging area for these units. These systems are checked and repaired, if necessary, at this facility prior to shipment to installation. Second, the facility provides the means for the design and evaluation of improvements to existing equipment or the development of new and more capable communications systems.

The Submarine Towed Array facility is used to design, develop, fabricate, test, and evaluate all aspects of towed array technology. Its function encompasses fundamental research for the development of new towed array and associated handling equipment, signal processing equipment, the setting and measurement of basic performance standards, and the test and evaluation of materials.

The Acoustic Warfare Laboratory consists of two main elements. The first is a complete AN/WLR-9A acoustic intercept receiver system. It allows design and evaluation of proposed system improvements prior to sea testing, thereby providing useful guidance on sea test design to maximize the collection of data. A precision tape playback facility provides a means for real time system stimulation using raw data recorded at sea, thereby reducing the amount of sea test time normally requested.

The Transducer Measurement Laboratory is an indoor tank facility used to develop and test transducers for sonar systems. Extensive acoustic, mechanical, and electrical measurements are taken here on transducers and associated composite structures and materials. It consists of a 15-foot-deep concrete measurement tank, lined with acoustic damping material and equipped with rails and carriages. Instrumentation includes an optical interferometer, a high-voltage dielectric test unit, a low-and high-temperature environmental chamber, a 10-KW power amplifier, and an AN/FQM-12 system prior to distribution of such modifications and upgrades Navy-wide.

The Chemistry Department applies quantitative analytical chemistry techniques; this Laboratory performs a variety of functions related to undersea systems. These include designing and building special molds and fixtures for submarine hull-mounted and towed array programs; assembling and materials (elastomers) e.g., for the Advanced Conformal Submarine Acoustic Sensor (ACSAS) array; various repairs to faulty transducers, such as for the Wide Aperture Array; quick fixes to the TR-155G rubber face and acoustic windows for experimental transducers; and developing and testing special adhesive systems for bonding external arrays to submarine hulls.

Chronology of Significant Events

1862	Goat Island occupied by the U.S. Naval Academy.
1865	Mooring built for frigates U.S.S. *Constitution* and U.S.S. *Santee*.
1869	Naval Torpedo Station established for the development of torpedoes, explosives and electrical equipment.
1870	Development of the first U.S. Navy Fish torpedo.
1871	Lt. John Howell, U.S.N., granted patent No. 121052 for his Howell torpedo.
1871	Counter-rotation propellers for torpedo propulsion patented.
1871	First test of the Fish torpedo.
1873	One Lay torpedo purchased for testing and evaluation.
1874	Development of the second-generation Fish torpedo.
1877	First hostile firing of a Whitehead Torpedo: H.M.S. *Shah* on Peruvian ironclad pirate ship was unsuccessful.
1878	Russian torpedo boats successfully launch Whitehead Torpedoes on Turkish ships.
1880	U.S. Navy discontinues issue of towing torpedoes.
1881	Systems for electric lighting aboard ships developed.
1882	Diving school established.
1886	U.S. Navy purchases U.S.S. *Stiletto*, prototype torpedo boat from Herreshoff Manufacturing Co.
1887	Electric lighting installed in all island buildings.
1888	Hotchkiss Ordnance Co., Providence, RI purchases rights to build the Howell torpedo.
1889	Hotchkiss receives order for 30 Howell torpedoes for U.S. Navy.
1890	First U.S. Navy torpedo boat, the *Cushing* is commissioned. Two 18-inch torpedo tubes installed.
1891	First capital ship sunk by a Whitehead Torpedo under wartime conditions.
1892	E. W. Bliss Co., gains rights to manufacture Whitehead Torpedo in United States.
1892	Bliss contracts for 100 Whitehead Mk-1 torpedoes for the U.S. Navy.
1893	Trainable mounts are installed on the TB-1 U.S.S. *Cushing's* torpedo tubes.
1894	Patent for steering gyro is granted.
1898	Captured Spanish Schwartzkopff torpedo arrives at Naval Torpedo Station for dissection.
1898	U.S. Navy purchases twelve Schwartzkopff torpedoes.
1898	Development of Whitehead 5-meter Mk-1 torpedo with gyro.

1899	Development of Whitehead 5-meter Mk-2 torpedo.
1900	First U.S. Navy submarine, the U.S.S. *Holland*, arrives at torpedo station for tests.
1901	Operated by U.S. Navy crew from the torpedo station, the *Holland* successfully gets within torpedo striking distance of the battleship U.S.S. *Kearsage* without detection.
1901	Development of use of smokeless powder for impulse launching from surface torpedo tubes.
1901	Development of Whitehead Mk-5 hot-running torpedoes with three-speed/range adjustment.
1901	First U.S. Navy torpedo boat destroyer, the DD-1 U.S.S. *Bainbridge* launched.
1904	Bliss-Leavitt Mk1 hot-running, vertical turbine torpedo development completed.
1905–1908	Development of Bliss-Leavitt Mk 2, Mk 3, and Mk 4 two-stage, vertical turbine driven, hot-running, torpedoes.
1907	First fully integrated torpedo factory erected on Goat Island.
1908	First Torpedo Station order received for Whitehead Mk 5 torpedoes.
1910	Seaman Gunner rating in U.S. Navy replaced by Torpedoman rating.
1911	Development of Bliss-Leavitt Mk 6 torpedo, horizontal turbine driven.
1911	Development of Bliss-Leavitt Mk 7 torpedo, first (so-called) steam torpedo.
1911	Development of Bliss-Leavitt Mk 8 torpedo for destroyer standard 21-inch torpedo tube.
1914	Anti-circular-run (ACR) mechanism warhead installation adopted.
1915	Development of Bliss-Leavitt Mk 9 and Mk 10 torpedo.
1915–1918	Development of Sperry electric torpedo. Unsuccessful.
1917	First flush deck, four-stack, destroyer with 12 21-inch torpedo tubes, the U.S.S. *Caldwell*.
1918	Gould Island in Narragansett Bay acquired by Navy as high-explosive storage site.
1920	Experimental torpedo launching from aircraft with torpedo Mk 7, Mod 5.
1921	Naval Torpedo Station Air Detail established at Gould Island.
1922	Battleship use of torpedoes discontinued.
1922	All torpedoes designed prior to torpedo Mk 7 withdrawn from use.
1923	All torpedo work at locations other than Goat Island terminated.
1923–1926	Development of torpedo Mk 11, selectable three-speed capability; the first all U.S. Navy design, started at Washington Navy Yard, completed by Naval Torpedo Station.
1927	Air blowing exercise head developed.
1928	Torpedo Mk 12 developed.
1930	Electric torpedo Mk 1, Type EL changed from 18-inch to 21-inch configuration.
1931	Bureau of Ordnance (BuOrd) purchase patents for Hammond radio-controlled torpedo.
1931	BuOrd canceled development of electric torpedo Mk 1, Type EL.
1931–1937	Development of torpedoes Mk 13 and Mk 14.
1936	Use of torpedoes on cruisers discontinued.
1940	Development of Naval torpedo Mk 17.
1941	Development of electric torpedo Mk 1 reactivated.
1942	German electric torpedo G7e taken from captured submarine U-57.
1942	Electric torpedo Mk 18 developed by Westinghouse Electric Corp., Sharon, PA.

1942	Development of torpedo Mk 19, electric control version of Mk 18, Westinghouse Electric.
1942–1943	Development of mine Mk 24, first acoustic homing antisubmarine weapon (ASW).
1942–1943	Development of mine Mk 23, parallel/backup development of mine Mk 24.
1942–1945	First active acoustic torpedo, the Mk 32 by General Electric Co., Pittsfield, MA.
1943	Electric torpedo Mk 2 designated torpedo Mk 20.
1943–1946	Development of aircraft/submarine-launched acoustic torpedo Mk 33.
1943	German submarines using T4 and T5 homing torpedoes.
1943	Mine Mk 24 credited with sinking German submarine U-160, July 1943.
1943	Development of torpedo Mk 27, Mod 0, submarine-launched version of Mine Mk 24.
1943	Development of torpedo Mk 16 Naval.
1943–1946	Development of torpedo Mk 25 to replace torpedo Mk 13.
1943	Development of aircraft-launched, passive-homing, electric torpedo Mk 21, Mod 0.
1943	Torpedo station develops torpedo Mk 23 and single-speed (high) version torpedo Mk 14.
1943–1945	Development of torpedo Mk 21 Mod 2 and passive homing torpedo Mk 13.
1944	Development of torpedo Mk 22; also fixed-depth, active acoustic homing electric torpedo.
1944	Development of torpedo Mk 26 and the seawater-activated battery.
1944	Development of passive homing, full-size electric torpedo Mk 28.
1944–1947	Development of torpedo Mk 29 an improved Mk 28.
1944–1950	Investigation wake homing as torpedo control system. Torpedo Mk 30 development.
1944–1946	Torpedo Mk 31, a high-speed, acoustic homing version of torpedo Mk 18.
1944–1945	Development of torpedo Mk 34 Mod 1, and the Mk 24 two-speed mine.
1944–1952	Universal passive/active acoustic homing electric torpedo Mk 36 development.
1945–1950	High-speed, long-range non-homing torpedo Mk 36.
1946–1954	Active/passive acoustic electric torpedo Mk 37.
1946	Torpedo Mk 27 Mod 4, an improved version of torpedo Mk 27 Mod 0.
1946	Development of torpedo Mk 38 deferred in favor of development of torpedo Mk 37.
1946–1951	Wire-guided, course correction torpedo Mk 39.
1946	High-speed aircraft torpedo Mk 40 development.
1949–1950	Mk 41 aircraft-launched version of torpedo Mk 35.
1949–1952	Development of pattern-running torpedo Mk 42, a multi-lab program.
1950–1952	Conversion of Mk 32 to active acoustic ASW torpedo Mk 32 Mod 2.
1950–1952	Development of lightweight electric, ASW torpedo Mk 43 Mod 1.
1953–1957	Second generation light-weight, ASW torpedo Mk 44.
1953–1957	Development of rocket-assisted torpedo (RAT).
1956–1962	Anti-Submarine Rocket System (ASROC).
1956	Torpedo Mk 43 Mod 3, improved Mk 43 Mod 1.
1957	Torpedo Mk 45 electric, seawater-activated battery, nuclear warhead (ASTOR).
1960	Third-generation, lightweight ASW torpedo Mk 46.
1970	Torpedo Mk 47 proposed and cancelled due to torpedo Mk 48 program.
1965–1974	Advanced submarine-launched, acoustic, thermal propulsion torpedo Mk 48.

Noteworthy Leaders

David Dixon Porter (1813–1891)
Promoted Naval Experimental Stations

Porter was the son of Commodore David Porter (1780–1843), who commanded the frigate *Essex* during the War of 1812. He was foster brother of David G. Farragut of Civil War fame. Porter's naval apprenticeship began at age 11 when he accompanied his father on a mission against pirates preying on West Indies (Caribbean) shipping. At age 14, he joined the Mexican Navy; but he was soon captured by Spaniards. Upon his release in 1829, he entered the U.S. Navy as a midshipman.

David Dixon Porter was instrumental in winning many victories during the Civil War. His record earned him thanks from Congress and his promotion to Rear Admiral. With all of Porter's war experiences, he strongly supported intensive naval training. In 1866, he was promoted to Vice Admiral and given superintendence of the Naval Academy. President Grant appointed him as an advisor to the Navy Department where he instituted administrative reforms. In 1870, he succeeded Farragut as Admiral and served on the board of inspection until his death.

Admiral Porter recognized the need for naval experimental stations to evaluate new technologies dealing with underwater explosives and electricity that had emerged during the Civil War.   When he learned about Whitehead's torpedo, he directed the Naval Torpedo Station to evaluate the new self-propelled underwater projectile.

William Barker Cushing (1842–1871)
Civil War Hero

William Barker Cushing was born in Delafield, Wisconsin on November 4, 1842, the fifth of seven children of Doctor Milton Buckingham Cushing and Mary Barker Smith. On September 25, 1857, Cushing became a cadet midshipman at the U.S. Naval Academy at Annapolis, Maryland.

Cushing was no scholar. In his second year at the academy, in a class of thirty-seven, he stood "3 in gunnery, 8 in ethics, 13 in astronomy and 9 in general order of merit and

APPENDIX B

Noteworthy Leaders

David Dixon Porter (1813–1891)
Promoted Naval Experimental Stations

Porter was the son of Commodore David Porter (1780–1843), who commanded the frigate *Essex* during the War of 1812. He was foster brother of David G. Farragut of Civil War fame. Porter's naval apprenticeship began at age 11 when he accompanied his father on a mission against pirates preying on West Indies (Caribbean) shipping. At age 14, he joined the Mexican Navy; but he was soon captured by Spaniards. Upon his release in 1829, he entered the U.S. Navy as a midshipman.

David Dixon Porter was instrumental in winning many victories during the Civil War. His record earned him thanks from Congress and his promotion to Rear Admiral. With all of Porter's war experiences, he strongly supported intensive naval training. In 1866, he was promoted to Vice Admiral and given superintendence of the Naval Academy. President Grant appointed him as an advisor to the Navy Department where he instituted administrative reforms. In 1870, he succeeded Farragut as Admiral and served on the board of inspection until his death.

Admiral Porter recognized the need for naval experimental stations to evaluate new technologies dealing with underwater explosives and electricity that had emerged during the Civil War.   When he learned about Whitehead's torpedo, he directed the Naval Torpedo Station to evaluate the new self-propelled underwater projectile.

William Barker Cushing (1842–1871)
Civil War Hero

William Barker Cushing was born in Delafield, Wisconsin on November 4, 1842, the fifth of seven children of Doctor Milton Buckingham Cushing and Mary Barker Smith. On September 25, 1857, Cushing became a cadet midshipman at the U.S. Naval Academy at Annapolis, Maryland.

Cushing was no scholar. In his second year at the academy, in a class of thirty-seven, he stood "3 in gunnery, 8 in ethics, 13 in astronomy and 9 in general order of merit and last in conduct." Cushing failed to graduate from Annapolis. His casual approach to discipline and academics was too disruptive. He was ordered to leave the Academy just months before his class graduated. He signed his forced resignation on March 23, 1861.

Cushing became an Acting Master's Mate in the United States Volunteer Navy, and was assigned to the U.S.S. *Minnesota*. After showing his mettle, Cushing quickly rose up the ladder from Midshipman to Ensign. The Civil War meant many opportunities for promotion. In August 1862, 19-year-old Cushing became a Lieutenant.

His personal heroism in sinking the Confederate ironclad the *Albemarle* in the Roanoke River in a steam launch armed only with a spar torpedo earned him a prominent place in naval history. Lt. Cushing proposed a small boat attack on the ironclad using boats of his own design. The Navy Department agreed, and sent the 21-year-old officer to New York to have the boats built. Once there, he obtained two 30 foot picket boats. Engineers outfitted the open steam launches with small, screw-propelled engines, 12-pounder howitzers mounted in their bows, and a complicated 14 foot torpedo hook (spar) securely bracketed to the sides of the launches. If the boom was extended properly, and the aiming lanyard and the trigger line properly manipulated, the 100 pounds of powder would detonate.

The success of Cushing's mission prompted the U.S. Navy's research and development of new generations of mines and torpedoes.

Robert Whitehead (1823–1905)
Inventor–the Automobile Torpedo

In the mid-1860s, Robert Whitehead, an English engineer working in Austria, created a radical new self-propelled (automobile) underwater missile that revolutionized naval warfare. His company, located in the Austrian port of Fiume (today's Rijeka) on the Adriatic Sea, developed a covert undersea weapon with a warhead that exploded below the waterline. It was the world leader in torpedo development and production up to the First World War. His invention caught the attention of the world's major naval powers, and Whitehead became wealthy building and selling torpedoes. Whitehead's automobile torpedo strongly influenced the evolution of the torpedo station on Newport's Goat Island. The first torpedoes produced by the U.S. Navy were Whitehead Mk 5 torpedoes built at the Naval Torpedo Station at the beginning of the 1900s.

Chester T. Minkler (1917–1952)
Inventor–the Depth Charge

Minkler as an ordnance engineer at the Naval Torpedo Station at Newport, Rhode Island, was one of the U.S. Navy's leading experts in explosives. He dedicated 44 years of experimentation and development to the Station. During this time, he established a solid reputation as father of the depth charge by perfecting a depth bomb, which proved to be more successful than any previous type.

Minkler developed a depth bomb which, when it sank into the ocean, was fired by a piston driven against the firing mechanism by the pressure of the water; the pressure mechanism was made adjustable to the depth at which the explosion occurred could be pre-determined. During the Second World War more than 40,000 of these weapons, known as "ash cans," were used, with devastating effect, against German U-boats.

Throughout his years at the Station, Minkler's talent and interests in experimenting with explosives led to many successes in developing underwater weapon technologies that were major milestones in undersea warfare for the U.S. Navy. During the Second World War, he developed a mechanism that regulated the torpedo's firing. This inventor's improvements to mines and torpedoes were vital to allied victories during both world wars.

Arthur C. Coogan (1897–1983)
Deputy Director–Naval Underwater Ordnance Station

Coogan's career began in 1919 when he was appointed to the Naval Torpedo Station as an Ordnance Draftsman. In 1934 he was promoted to Chief Tool and Gauge Designer. Because of his extensive knowledge of production methods, in 1936 Coogan was promoted to Factory Manager.

After the Second World War, Coogan became Civilian Manager of the Station. Beginning in 1953, as Deputy Director, Coogan was the senior civilian responsible for managing and overseeing the transition of the Torpedo Station during the crucial post-Second World War period. He directed engineering efforts in the technical departments, carried out vital administrative functions, and formulated policies and procedures in the running of a research and development laboratory.

Grace Herreshoff's 1902 Torpedo Station Narrative

After a visit to the Torpedo Station in 1902, Grace Herreshoff wrote the following monograph about her impression of Goat Island and the Torpedo Station. It was published in *The New England Magazine*, volume 32, 1902, pages 167-181 with twelve photographs. Herreshoff's narrative is particularly interesting for her description of the torpedoes and her observations on the Station.

As our late war with Spain has quickened the interest and increased the activity in our new Navy, so the greater Civil War set on foot more ambitious projects and offered wider opportunities for inventions, "changing the old order and giving place to the new." A wonderfully able Navy was that of the sixties; but one of the most essential elements the present day organization possesses, it lacked: the torpedo, which, previous to the Civil War, was in the most embryonic state, needing the activity of actual warfare to bring it into prominent notice. In the general revitalization of all governmental departments, a spirit engendered by the final demonstration of the Nation's power, attention was turned to the powerful explosives then recently brought into use by the Navy, and the subject seeming to open up unknown possibilities, it was thought wise to pursue a special course of study and experiment upon torpedoes. To this end, Admiral Porter selected, as the home of the Torpedo Station, Goat Island, forming one of the protections of the harbor of Newport, Rhode Island, convenient to and yet removed a safe distance from the city. The little island—it is hardly a mile and a half long—was the property of the Army, however, and had hitherto been known only for its disused Fort Wolcott, where the Naval Academy boys had been drilled during wartime: but Admiral Porter's scheme was too excellent to pass unnoticed, and the value of Goat Island was fixed at $50,000, a yearly rental of $5,000 being decided upon.

Accordingly, on July 29, 1869, the island was transferred from the War to the Navy Department, only by lease, however, for the possession of anything so stable as dry land is denied those whose domain covers all the seas of the earth; a Torpedo corps was organized, under the direction of Commander E. O. Matthews, as Inspector in Charge, took possession of Goat Island in September. Until the routine should be regularly established and adequate working space provided, the old army barracks were transformed into lecture rooms and laboratories, while a machine shop and storehouse were evolved from the few shelters the naval cadets has left behind.

The Naval Torpedo Station's headquarters for the Inspector in Charge.

One of the first research buildings built at the Station was the electrical laboratory.

During the first five years of the station's growth, were erected its most important buildings, which are those in present use; they were the machine shop, store house, electric and chemical laboratories, several cottages for the officers, and the inspector's house, which latter was built over the old barracks and includes also various offices. In 1881, a comparatively large guncotton factory was built on the west shore, and for a period of years that explosive was manufactured exclusively at Goat Island, though of late only a small quantity for experimental use is yearly turned out. It being found impracticable to mass in one building so great a quantity of sensitive explosives—the factory was destroyed by fire, with some loss of life, in 1893—a number of small buildings were erected along the west shore, and built into the embankment that was cut out to receive them. This scheme was rendered the more necessary by the introduction of smokeless powder into general use. In each little building, only one-step in the transformation of the raw cotton can be effected, thus reducing to a minimum the danger of explosion.

Goat Island, or the Torpedo Station, as it is invariably called, is entirely surrounded by a heavy seawall of stone and masonry, begun under the direction of Captain, then Commander Converse; and it was only by the timely construction of this barrier that the island was saved from the uselessness to which the constant wear of the waves threatened to reduce it. From its northernmost point—Goat Island, long and narrow, extends almost due north and south—a heavy stone breakwater stretches some one thousand six hundred feet up the bay, ending in a lighthouse of the usual neat, white-plastered variety. Both the breakwater and Goat Island Light were built long before the creation of the Torpedo Station—about 1840. In fact, while even previous to that date a small light was maintained on the point, its keeper inhabiting a house nearby.

The aspect which the station presents, as one approaches it on a summer's day, is not without its beauty; with the winter days it is best not to concern one's self, for then the bleak winds, sweeping up and down the bay, seem to render even one's foothold insecure. In the summer, the ground is grass-covered; the vines embellish the six severely plain cottages, marshalled [*sic*] in a row along the south part of the island occupied by the officers constituting the personnel of the station. Even a few tenderly cared for trees flourish before the commandant's quarters directly opposite the landing-pier, though elsewhere the neatly marked path and roads gleam white in the sunlight. And let it here be noted that the extreme neatness prevalent at the Torpedo Station is such as to remind one forcibly of the "holystoned" and orderly appearance of a great battleship. Over in front of the machine shop a number of ponderous torpedoes and tubes of obsolete make, with other objects of that nature, are regularly disposed on the lawn, and clumsy old submarine mines (one "ancient" example is dated 1880, such is the haste of modern invention!) mark the corners of the paths.

And here, north of the inspector's quarters and scattered over the widest part of the island, within and about the embankments of the old fort, stands the little group of buildings which shelter the forces that go to make up the Torpedo Station—that little speck on the great map of the United States which exercises on the Navy an influence out of all proportion to its size. For the purpose of the Torpedo Station is to manufacture, instruct, and primarily to experiment. Every invention of use to the Navy, except in the line of propelling machinery and heavy armament or "ordnance proper," passes through or has its birth at the station. Here also a large number of officers and men receives instruction on matters of vital importance.

As the Station advanced in torpedo research and development, the most important structure in accomplishing the task was the machine shop. Pictured on the grounds of the machine shop are torpedoes and torpedo tubes taken from Spanish ships at Santiago.

A *c.* 1900 view of the Station's administration building (left) and the nearby machine shop.

Though guncotton and smokeless powder are no longer manufactured exclusively at the Station, there are produced here the primers and fuses, exploders and detonators, which fire the charges of guns and torpedoes; and the power, which these insignificant objects possess, is symbolical of the importance of the Torpedo Station. They are, generally speaking, small round receptacles of brass, one or two inches in length, filled in the case of primers and fuses, which ignite gun powder, with a very fine meal powder; but the contents of exploders and detonators, which explode the guncotton in a torpedo and are of necessity more powerful, are composed mainly of fulminate of mercury. A recent invention at the Station is the combination primer, which as the name indicates, unites in one primer the forces of two different classes; so that if, say the electricity, should fail to act, the charge will still be fired by virtue of the power of friction which the primer also possesses—and vice versa.

On the floor above the machine shop is the torpedo lecture room, a large hall in which officers and men are instructed, fairly lined with torpedoes, most of which are the modern automobiles: but in one corner hang three obsolete forms, one of which possesses an historic interest in having been taken from the Spanish warship *Maria Teresa*. The Whitehead automobiles, however, predominate in interest, for they are the torpedoes in common use at the present time. The Howell—also an automobile—is occasionally used, to be sure, and is most successful in actual warfare; but its delicate and complex mechanism (it is propelled by a revolving disc instead of by compressed air, as is the Whitehead) renders it impracticable for instruction or "exercise" use.

The modern torpedo is a cylindrical case of steel, 11 feet 8 inches, or 15 feet long (the Whitehead is used in two sizes) and nearly 18 inches at its greatest diameter, tapering to the bluntly rounded "head" at one end and to the slender pointed "tail," carrying the rudder and propellers, at the other. Into three sections is the wonderful torpedo divided: the head, holding the explosive; the air flask—which is the middle section—containing the driving power of air at a high pressure; and the after body in which are the engine, shaft and steering gear, together with various appliances controlling the idiosyncrasies of this miniature submarine vessel. For such the torpedo really seems to be guiding itself, and entirely independent of any outside agency from the time it leaves the tube, until the little war-nose projecting from the head touches a solid substance, when the guncotton with which the warhead is packed explodes and the torpedo, with its target is blown to atoms.

But in carrying out its purpose of destruction upon the opposing force what an exquisite piece of workmanship is sacrificed in the torpedo! Its interior is filled with numerous delicate and complicated mechanisms, which automatically regulate its course, every possible contingency being provided for.

That it may the more resemble an actual boat, one small compartment is called the engine room; within this the little engine, occupying a space hardly a foot in diameter and driven by the force of compressed air, accomplishes thirteen hundred revolutions per minute. Though racing at this tremendous rate, it can and does stop on the instant without injuring in the slightest, without even jarring the delicate machinery surrounding it. The speed made by this miniature ship in passing through the water, which, it must be remembered, offers resistance to its entire surface is twenty-six knots per hour for a run of eight hundred yards, and amounts to about thirty knots when half the distance is to be covered. As a matter of comparison, let it be noted that the engines of the torpedo boat *Dupont*, gigantic in contrast to the dainty mechanism under consideration, cannot make more than four hundred revolutions per minute, yet with this power the boat, encountering to be sure, less resistance can make over twenty-eight knots per hour—nearly the greatest speed of which the torpedo is capable. What, then, would be the speed of the *Dupont*, could her powerful engines, without destroying themselves, even approach the high rate reached by a torpedo's machinery!

As torpedoes are in constant use for both instruction and experiment, it would of course be dangerous and even impossible for them always to carry their charge of guncotton, accordingly each is provided, besides the warhead, with an exercise head, which is filled with water, in order that its weight may equal that of the former.

A torpedo is fired from a tube, the upper half of which projects, roof-like over the mouth, as a shell from a gun, that is by a charge of powder ignited by a primer; but with this difference, that the torpedo travels under its own propelling power, whereas the shell gains its momentum from the force of the ejecting charge. It requires, however, great care and skill to set correctly the different regulators in a torpedo, preparatory to the run, and it is both interesting and ludicrous to watch the proceeding of the novices at "target practice," for they are prone to forget the most important adjustments.

A "surface run" is most remarkable to witness, then the huge cigar-shaped object goes skimming across the water, occasionally leaping several feet into the air, looking and behaving exactly like a porpoise. While making a great rushing and whirring noise, like the sound of a train speeding through a tunnel, a fact not at all strange when one remembers that the fifteen-foot torpedo is running at a rate of twenty-six to thirty knots. Perhaps the steering gear is left to its own devices immediately the torpedo proceeds upon a course most bewildering and even terrifying to the beholder; turning in circles, running up against some object only to be headed off in another direction, and, when the compressed air is finally exhausted, describing an arc in the air before ending its gyrations at the most unexpected spot. Occasionally a torpedo will be lost, burying itself in the mud or following so eccentric a course beneath the water evading the vigilance of the searchers: but it is usually recovered eventually, as was the case with a torpedo found recently by divers under instruction at the Station. Though having lain a year and five days beneath the water, it was found to be intact, and will perhaps be used eighty or a hundred times for exercise purposes during its future existence.

It is hardly possible to realize that this remarkable mechanism is the result of so humble a beginning as the primitive spar torpedo. This explosive, it can hardly be called a missile, came into existence about the time of the Civil War, and was nothing more than a cast iron box filled with coarse gun powder, and fastened to the end of a long spar, or "boom," which was carried alongside a launch, though projecting some distance in front of the bow. As this torpedo could not be exploded until the launch was beside the object of attack, and as this act was accomplished by means of a primitive friction primer, manipulated by a cord, the danger to the operators was nearly as great as to the enemy. Though spar torpedoes have been superseded by automobiles they have been constantly improved: the shell is now of steel, the charge has become guncotton ignited by an electric detonator. At a recent experiment in the waters near Goat Island, four of these modern spar torpedoes were exploded, sending great beams of wood two hundred feet into the air, while the solid column of smoke and debris seemed to extend unto the clouds themselves.

The next step from the spar was the towing torpedo, dragged by careful manipulation of two lines at some distance off the quarter of a vessel, and made to dive beneath her adversary. An approach to the automobiles were the Lay, Lay-Haite, Ericsson, and the Edison-Simms torpedoes; but these, although propelled by their own power were hampered by the cables controlling them from a boat or shore. In 1870, before the adoption of the Whitehead by the our Navy the so-called Station torpedo, resembling the English one was constructed and experimented with at the island; it gave way, however to the Howell, which though a later invention was introduced here at about the same time as the Whitehead, the most recent, and by all odds, the best.

It is a remarkable, and perhaps not fully realized coincidence, that during the Spanish War not a single torpedo was fired by our vessels, the torpedo boats having been mainly used as despatch boats, defending themselves when necessary, with small guns with which they were provided. Consequently, the first explosion of a Whitehead under actual conditions of war took place only in 1900, in Narragansett Bay, when the United States Torpedo Boat *Porter*, running at full speed, fired a torpedo at a distance of eight hundred yards from the target, the beach at Prudence Island. Then immediately turned about and fled to a safe distance. Several other torpedoes boats were assembled, with a number of officers on board to witness the experiment, which resulted most satisfactorily, effectually proving that with the discharge of a single torpedo the *Porter* could destroy the enemy's ship and herself escape with practically no damage.

Mines were originally intended to receive as much attention at the Station as torpedoes, but shortly after its beginning the mine department was removed to Willet's Point, not however before Captain Converse had made an important invention in that line. The Naval Defense mines are invariably loaded at the Station, and at the time of the Spanish War, the employees were kept busy filling the countermines.

Not only are mines and torpedoes loaded there, but also it is at the Torpedo Station that the torpedo outfit of every vessel in the Navy is assembled; and on-going out of commission it is there a ship returns her outfit, to be repaired or if necessary, replaced. The regulations, moreover, provide that an overhauling of the outfit shall take place every three years. With the "rush in business" entailed by the tremendous growth of the Navy during recent years, it is not surprising to find the payroll of the employees at the Torpedo Station increased from about $100 per month in 1872, to about $400 per day in 1902.

The experiment maneuvers at the island are by no means confined to torpedoes. Back of the machine shop stands the electrical laboratory, a neat little building crowned by the searchlight tower, in which is given practical instruction on this weapon of the new Navy. In the lecture rooms are to be found examples of every kind of electric light used on board a vessel, from the huge search light, down to the minute one-half candle power incandescent, with which the inside of a torpedo is illuminated for examination. The dynamo room is also the place of particular investigation and practical instruction to both officers and men.

Leaving the electric laboratory, one approaches an archway cut through the high embankment, which formerly surrounded the fort; one approaches, but may not pass through, for within the enclosure stand two buildings closed to the outside world. The larger is the chemical laboratory, in which are conducted experiments in the line of explosives; in the small building to the right of the entrance the blocks of wet guncotton are shaped, by means of a circular saw, to fit snugly into the oval warheads. Sawing guncotton sounds as if it were a decidedly hazardous proceeding; but as the material is saturated with water and every possible precaution taken, the workmen are nearly as safe as are those in the machine shop—more so than the workers on detonators, perhaps, for a careless blow, be it ever so light, on the sensitive fulminator may result in the serious, if not fatal, wounding of the workman.

In one wall of the white plastered archway is cut the name of the French engineer, very modestly, "Rochefontain Enginr." He it was who threaded the embankments with passages, partly underground; leading into these are little doors at intervals in the walls, one of which, in a corner of the enclosure opens into an old prison in the tunnel.

Again, back of the enclosure is another, but solid embankment, which extends thence along the west shore nearly to the breakwater; it is this embankment that shelters the six guncotton and smokeless powder houses, entrance into which, it is hardly necessary to state, is strictly forbidden.

Buildings 1, 2 and 3 comprise the guncotton factory. In the first of these the raw cotton is picked apart and dried; a certain brand of English cotton being always used, as it is the most successfully treated in the manufacture of the powder. The second step is the nitrate bath, out of which the cotton, now nitrocellulose, is wrung and washed, then carried to building 3 to be reduced to a soft pulp; after a final wringing the guncotton is ready to be taken to building 4, which, with 5 and 6, is the smokeless powder factory. From building 4, the cotton emerges transformed into smokeless powder, and having the appearance of sticks of glue; but a process of drying and seasoning, accomplished in the next building, is now necessary, and after that the powder undergoes a final test, lying stored in the last building under different degrees of temperature before it is issued for use.

The preparation to which the guncotton is subjected, the ingredients of which are known to very few, is of course constantly experimented upon and, as the results show, greatly improved, for the smokeless powder of the present day has obtained a considerable advance in velocity over that of a few years ago. Many of the experiments in the action of guncotton and smokeless powder of the present day are conducted on Rose Island, which lies to the north-west of the Station, and where a guncotton magazine is also situated. The subject of nearly as much study as the powder itself is the elimination of danger from explosion during its manufacture, and of disease to the workmen; and to that end, the buildings have been constructed so they may be frequently and thoroughly cleansed while some progress has been made in protecting the men from the "noxious vapors" arising from the chemicals.

As a place of instruction, the Torpedo Station holds a position of importance in the Navy. Not only are classes of officers engaged there every summer in practical study on torpedo work, electricity, the chemistry of explosives, etc., but each year two classes of seamen, the pick of the enlisted men, are thoroughly trained in electricity and torpedo work, and, if they so desire and are physically fit, in diving. The course in torpedoes renders the men capable not only to fire the missiles, but also to give them proper care and repair when disabled. A lasting proof of the excellence of the Station's diving course was furnished by the work and condition of the men diving on the wreck of the *Maine* in Havana Harbor. So thorough had been their physical training, that after 50 days of continuous work in the filth and stench of the harbor, in a hot and oppressive climate, not one of the naval divers suffered any ill effects or was in any way injured—a most unusual occurrence in any wrecking company. As to their ability, though the New York press was at first inclined to criticize, comparing the "sailors" unfavorably with the professional divers, at the last it was eager to admit their undoubted skill and bravery.

With their previous six months' training in the gun-shops at the Washington Navy Yard, the men qualify as seamen gunners after this seventeen weeks' course, and are usually ordered at once to sea; later those who exhibit sufficient ability rise to the rank of warrant officers.

A small portion of their time of study at the Station is spent on board torpedo boats, the men thus becoming somewhat accustomed to sea duty, though of course the majority are sent on board battleships and cruisers, gunboats, and other smaller vessels, whose numbers predominate over those of torpedo boats. Life on the latter, it must be understood, is quite a different matter from that on any other ship in the Navy. In the first place, torpedo boats are not built for men to live on; far less with a view to comfort; in fact the question of existence on board was so far forgotten in the cases of the *Craven* and *Dahlgren* that no spaces were allowed for the galleys, and on their completion it was necessary to construct them between the stacks on deck! It is however, well known that these boats were not the result of American talent.

Beyond the primary purpose of discharging her missiles, the objects of a torpedo boat are facility of control and speed, speed that will enable her to outstrip any other class of vessel whatsoever; save only the torpedo boat destroyers, which are merely torpedo boats raised to a higher power, size, armament, and speed increased, but not altered. But to attain this speed a torpedo boat must be of a slender shape and lie low on the water, in order to escape observation as well as to offer the least possible resistance; further she must not be uselessly encumbered with elaborate fittings, but every portion of her make-up must be reduced to the least weight,

Torpedo boats moored in Newport Harbor allow the viewer to appreciate the nearness of the city of Newport to Goat Island. *Left to right:* the torpedo boats are: the *Winslow*, the *Stiletto*, the *Morris*, and the *Dupont*. *Official U.S. Navy photograph*

while her machinery must embody in a compact form a tremendous amount of power. Fully as elevated as her speed qualifications must be her ability to respond to the lightest touch on the wheel, to reverse, stop, or start her engines at a second's notice; for she depends in battle not upon the material protection of heavy armor plate, which would weigh her down and detract from her swiftness, but upon her own insignificance and cunning in escape.

A torpedo boat is in proportion to her size, without exception the fastest vessel afloat. Though the *Dupont* is but 175 feet in length, with a displacement of 165 tons, her 3,800 horse power of her engines is equal to that of the Sound liners, such as the *Plymouth*, for instance, a boat of vastly greater tonnage and perhaps 150 feet longer. Yet the *Plymouth*'s speed is hardly two-thirds that of the torpedo boat. A comparison with a modern ocean liner, whose proportions more nearly approach those of a torpedo boat, is also interesting. Roughly speaking, the *Deutschland*—fastest of the ocean greyhounds—measures about four times the *Dupont*'s length and breadth; but against a hundredfold increase of tonnage, the *Deutschland* can develop only a nine times greater horse power, with the result that her speed lacks about five knots of the *Dupont*'s. The latter craft, be it noted, was built to attain a speed of twenty-six knots; but on her official trial, she exceeded the contract speed by two and one-half knots.

The power of endurance against the ceaseless battery of the waves and ice in our northern waters is not considered one of the requisites of a torpedo boat; but the *Dupont* with the smaller *Morris* refuted the idea that these diminutive vessels must be hauled out of the water or sent south during cold weather. Both of these boats successfully weathered the hard winter of 1898–99, moored to a dock in a sheltered cove of Bristol, Rhode Island Harbor; the *Dupont* going there directly after the terrible November storm of that season, while the *Morris* joined her later—in good time, however, to pass through the novel experience of being frozen in the ice for many weeks. But though the boats stood the test well, the crews endured untold discomforts.

Two members of the latter, nevertheless, seemed to enjoy life in the cold weather to which they were so unaccustomed. Both of southern birth, they were "Chic," the lively little fox terrier mascot of the *Morris* captured from some Spanish merchant ship: and "Dupont Bill," basely kidnapped in infancy from his Cuban home, a goat which gladly devoured the candy, with its paper bag, so frequently offered him by the sailors, as well on one occasion, the feathers decorating a visitor's hat! For a short time last winter, the *McKee* was rejoiced with "Bill's" presence as a guest, and it was on one of her trips that he narrowly escaped a watery grave. The trip was memorable on the boat's career as well as in "Billy's."

The *McKee*, which is the smallest of her class—hardly one hundred feet in length and of only sixty-five tons displacement—left New York one stormy day for Newport, expecting to arrive in about eight hours. A short distance along the Sound, however, her blowers gave out and she was forced to proceed under natural draft, crawling along at about three knots an hour, while the seas literally swept over her, nearly sweeping poor "Billy" overboard. At last he was lashed to the smokestack, and though half smothered by the water, weathered the twenty-four hour nightmare of a trip; meanwhile the executive officer, "Bill's" only companion on deck, was forced to grasp the supporting stack in a close embrace.

Innumerable are these unofficial records of runs bravely accomplished under conditions with which no torpedo boat was designed to cope: but so enjoyable can warm, fair weather render a short trip, that one would forever scorn the most luxurious steam yacht after a single rapid, exhilarating run on a torpedo boat.

The *McKee* has been mentioned as the smallest vessel of her class. Still smaller is the *Stiletto*, the only wood torpedo boat in the Navy; be the other slips crowded or deserted, she is always to be found at her dock at the Torpedo Station. Moored near last summer, was that representative of a new type, the submarine torpedo boat—*Holland*; and very strange and weird, like some deep sea monster newly dragged into the light of day, appeared that part of her fifty feet of length visible when she rises to the surface. As far as the question of life on board (or is it within?) is concerned, the *Holland* is a little more comfortable than a diving suit, and can be stored with sufficient air and food to support her crew of five for forty-eight hours; as to the question of destruction upon an outside force, this submarine vessel is an undoubted success, as was proved in the fleet and harbor defense maneuvers held at Newport the last summer. It was reported on this occasion, that the *Holland* could have "torpedoed" (synonymous with "destroyed") probably three ships of the blockading fleet. In strange juxtaposition to this modern invention, an old submarine boat designed by Admiral Porter, lies near the docks at the station. It is a box-like structure of iron, divided within into compartments, one of which contains an ancient smooth-bore gun, and intended to be sunk to a stationary position.

It has been almost entirely through the ceaseless activity of its many excellent commandants and assisting officers that the Torpedo Station has attained its prestige. The present Inspector is Commander N. E. Mason, the well-known executive officer of the U.S.S. *Brooklyn* during the Spanish War, who distinguished himself at Santiago; Lieutenant Commander Rees, formerly executive officer of the island, but ordered to sea duty August, 1901, most ably performed the duties of executive officer on no less a ship than the *Olympia* at Manila, under Admiral Dewey. It is hardly necessary to add that the Department strenuously endeavors to appoint the personnel of the Station from among the most active and efficient officers of the Navy.

Many years ago Rear Admiral Sampson was Inspector at the Station; and little known to the general public. With the increase of the new navy he has come into prominence, and by his ability has shown to the world her power in war—a power the growth of which is typified by the progress made at our Navy's Torpedo Station.

Civilian technicians from the Torpedo Station evaluate the performance of a Howell Mk 1 launched from the anchored torpedo boat TB14 *Morris* in Newport Harbor by a crew of Navy torpedo gunners. *1892 U.S.N. photo*

Coaster's Harbor Island and the Naval War College

In 1882, the Newport Poor House and Farm on the 92-acre Coasters Harbor Island were conveyed to the United States Navy by the City of Newport and the following year the gift was approved by the State of Rhode Island. This was done on the condition that the site be used for the training of recruits.

On June 4, 1883, the U.S. Naval Training Station was formally established; this eventually evolved into the Naval Education and Training Center (NETC). The Naval War College was established on Coasters Harbor Island a year later. It was originally located in a recently vacated public asylum. Since the fleet was not located near the College, the school had to come up with some method to test theories and concepts. Thus was what we now call "war gaming" born. War gaming continues to be part of the College's curriculum.

The College was established by Navy Department General Order No. 325 of 6 October 1884 through the efforts of Rear Admiral Stephen B. Luce, U.S.N., its first president. An ardent modernizer, Luce was responsible for significant developments in education and training. His most enduring single contribution is the Naval War College, described as "a place of original research on all questions relating to war and to statesmanship connected with war, or the prevention of war."

Annual Congressional Naval Appropriation Laws

Forty-Seventh Congress, Second Session—March 3, 1883

Torpedoes: For the purchase and manufacture, after full investigation and test in the United States under the direction of the Secretary of the Navy, of torpedoes adapted to naval warfare, or of the right to manufacture the same and for the fixtures and machinery necessary for operating the same, one hundred thousand dollars: *Provided*, No part of said money shall be expended for the purchase or manufacture of any torpedoes or of the right to manufacture the same until the same shall have been approved by the Secretary of the Navy, after a favorable report to be made to him by a board of naval officers to be created by him to examine and test said torpedoes and inventions.

Forty-Eighth Congress, Second Session—January 30, 1884

Bureau of Ordnance: For procuring, producing, and preserving ordnance material; for the torpedo corps, namely; for labor, material, freight and express charges; general repairs to grounds, buildings, and wharves; boats; instruction; instruments, tools, furniture, experiments, and general torpedo outfits, twenty-five thousand dollars.

Forty-Eighth Congress, Second Session—March 3, 1885

Bureau of Ordnance: For the torpedo corps, namely; for labor, material, freight and express charges; general repairs to grounds, buildings, and wharves; boats; instruction; instruments, tools, furniture, experiments, and general torpedo outfits, sixty thousand dollars.

Forty-Ninth Congress, Second Session—March 3, 1887

Bureau of Ordnance: Torpedo Station, Newport, Rhode Island: for one chemist, at two thousand five hundred dollars; one clerk, at one thousand two hundred dollars; one draughtsman, at one thousand five hundred dollars; in all, twenty-four thousand three hundred and forty-two dollars and twenty-five cents. And no other fund appropriated by this act shall be used in payment for such services.

Torpedo Corps: For labor, material, freight and express charges; general repairs to grounds, buildings, and wharves; boats; instruction; instruments, tools, furniture, experiments, and general torpedo outfits, fifty thousand dollars; extension to electrical laboratory, three thousand dollars; pontoon, eight hundred dollars; repairs to sea-wall, three thousand dollars; water-pipe from Newport to station one thousand dollars; in all, fifty-seven thousand eight hundred dollars.

To enable the Secretary of the navy to purchase the steamer *Stiletto* for use as a torpedo boat for experimental purposes, twenty-five thousand dollars.

Fiftieth Congress, First Session—September 7, 1888.

Training Station, Coasters' Harbor Island, Rhode Island: For repairs and improvement on buildings at Coasters' harbor island; heating, lighting, and furniture for same; books and stationary; freight and other contingent expenses; purchase of feed and maintenance of horses and mail-wagons, and attendance on same; and to enable the naval war college to be conducted at said Island up to January first, eighteen hundred and eighty-nine, ten thousand dollars.

Torpedo Station, Newport, Rhode Island: For one chemist, at two thousand five hundred dollars; on clerk, at one thousand two hundred dollars; one draughtsman, at one thousand five hundred dollars; in all twenty-four thousand five hundred and twenty-five dollars. And, no other fund appropriated by this act shall be used in payment for such service.

Torpedo Corps: for labor, material, freight, and express charges; general care of and repairs to grounds, buildings, wharves, and general torpedo outfits, fifty thousand dollars; new landing stage, seven hundred dollars; quarters for surgeons, eight thousand dollars; for correcting the sanitary conditions of the cottages used as quarters at the station, five thousand dollars; in all, sixty-five thousand seven hundred dollars.

Bureau of Provisions and Clothing—Torpedo Station, Newport: In general store house: one clerk, one thousand two hundred dollars.

Fiftieth Congress, Second Session—March 2, 1889.

Naval Torpedo Station and War College: for labor, material, freight, and express charges; general care of and repairs to grounds, buildings, and wharves; boats, instructions; instruments, tools, furniture, experiments, general torpedo outfits, and maintenance of the Naval Torpedo Station and War College on Goat Island, seventy thousand dollars.

For the construction of a building for use by the Naval Torpedo Station and War College as consolidated by order of the Secretary of the navy January eleventh, eighteen hundred and eighty-nine, one hundred thousand dollars, to be immediately available, said sum to be in full for all expenses of designing, erecting, and furnishing said building.

For enlarging torpedo boat house, five thousand dollars.

In general, store house: one clerk, at one thousand two hundred dollars.

Fifty-First Congress, First Session—June 30, 1890.

Naval Torpedo School and War College: for maintenance of the Naval War College and Torpedo School on Coaster's Harbor Island, ten thousand dollars; and the Secretary of the Navy is hereby authorized to cause the building for use by the Naval War College and Torpedo School, for the construction of which the sum of one hundred thousand dollars was appropriated in the act of March second, eighteen hundred and eighty-nine, to be erected on Coaster's Harbor Island.

Torpedo Station, Newport, Rhode Island: for labor, material, freight, and express charges; general care of and repairs to grounds, buildings, and wharves; boats, implements, tools, furniture, experiments and general torpedo outfits; sixty thousand dollars.

Increase of the Navy: one swift torpedo cruiser of about seven hundred and fifty ton displacement, at a cost, exclusive of armament, not to exceed three hundred and fifty thousand dollars, to have a maximum speed of not less than twenty-three knots; and one torpedo boat, at a cost not to exceed one hundred and twenty-five thousand dollars.

Fifty-First Congress, Second Session—March 2, 1891.

Torpedo Station, Newport, Rhode Island: for labor, material, freight, and express charges; general care of and repairs to grounds, buildings, and wharves; boats, implements, tools, furniture, experiments and general torpedo outfits; sixty thousand dollars.

Naval Torpedo Station, Newport, Rhode Island: for one chemist, at two thousand five hundred dollars; one clerk, at one thousand two hundred dollars; one draughtsman, at one thousand five hundred dollars.

Fifty-Second Congress, Second Session—March 3, 1893.

Submarine Torpedo Boat: For building a submarine torpedo boat and conduction experiments therewith, two hundred thousand dollars, to be taken from the balances of appropriations on hand July first, eighteen hundred and ninety-three, to the credit of armor and armament of vessels heretofore authorized.

Naval Torpedo Station: for one chemist, at two thousand five hundred dollars; on clerk at one thousand two hundred dollars; one draftsman, at one thousand five hundred dollars.

Naval War College and Torpedo School on Coasters Harbor Island: For maintenance of the naval War College and Torpedo School on Coasters Harbor Island and care of grounds for same, eight thousand dollars.

Fifty-Third Congress, Second Session—July 26, 1894.

Torpedo Station, Bureau of Ordnance, Newport, Rhode Island: for labor, material, freight, and express charges; general care of and repairs to grounds, buildings, and wharves; boats instructions, instruments, tools, furniture, experiments, and general torpedo outfits, sixty thousand dollars;

For replacing the gun-cotton factory destroyed by fire July third, eighteen hundred and ninety-three, eleven thousand and seventy-seven dollars.

For one chemist, at two thousand five hundred dollars; one clerk, at one thousand two hundred dollars; one draftsman, at one thousand five hundred dollars; in all five thousand two hundred dollars.

The Secretary of the Navy, is hereby authorized to use the four hundred and fifty thousand dollars "for the construction of one additional cruiser of the [pneumatic dynamite] *Vesuvius* type," appropriated by the Act of March second, eighteen hundred and eighty-nine, or so much thereof as may be necessary for the construction, armament, and equipment of three torpedo boats, to cost, all together, not more than the said sum of four hundred and fifty thousand dollars.

Fifty-Third Congress, Third Session—March 2, 1895.

Increase of the Navy: ... and in each case the contract shall be awarded by the Secretary of the navy to the lowest best responsible bidder; and three torpedo boats, at a cost of not exceeding one hundred and seventy-five thousand dollars each; and subject to the provisions hereinafter made, one seagoing battle ship and one of said torpedo boats shall be built on or near the coast of the Pacific Ocean, or in the waters connecting therewith, and one torpedo boat on the Mississippi river, and one torpedo boat on the coast of the gulf of Mexico; and in the construction of all said vessels all of the provisions of the Act of August third, eighteen hundred and eighty six.

Fifty-Fourth Congress, First Session—June 10, 1896.

Bureau of Ordnance: Reserve supply of projectiles for ships of the Navy, two hundred and fifty thousand dollars; reserve supply of torpedoes, one hundred and forty-two thousand dollars.

Torpedo Station, Newport, Rhode Island: For labor, material, freight, and express charges; general care of and repairs to grounds, buildings, and wharves; boats instructions, instruments, tools, furniture, experiments, and general torpedo outfits, sixty thousand dollars; for extending the sea wall, fifteen thousand dollars.

Increase of the Navy: For the purpose of further increasing the naval establishment of the United States the President is hereby authorized to have constructed ... three torpedo boats, to have a maximum speed of not less than thirty knots, to cost in all not exceeding eight hundred thousand dollars, and not to exceed ten torpedo boats to cost in all not exceeding five hundred thousand dollars, and to have the highest practicable speed for vessels of their class; and not more than two of said battleships and not more than three of said torpedo boats shall be built in one yard or by one contracting party, and in each case the contract shall be awarded by the Secretary of the Navy to the lowest responsible bidder; and in the construction of all said vessels all of the provisions of the Act of August third, eighteen hundred and eighty- six.

The Secretary of the Navy is hereby authorized to contract for the building of two submarine torpedo boats of the Holland type at a cost not exceeding one hundred and seventy-five thousand dollars each.

Fifty-Fourth Congress, Second Session—March 3, 1897.

Bureau of Ordnance Newport Torpedo Station: …continuing extension of sea wall, five thousand dollars; enlarging boiler house and two new boilers six thousand five hundred dollars.

For the purpose of further increasing the naval establishment of the United States the President is hereby authorized to have constructed by contract not more than three torpedo boats, to have a speed of not less than thirty knots, to cost in all not exceeding eight hundred thousand dollars, and not to exceed ten torpedo boats to cost in all not exceeding five hundred thousand dollars, and to have the highest practicable speed for vessels of their class; and not more than two of said torpedo boats shall be built in one yard or by one contracting party, and in each to the lowest best responsible bidder.

Fifty-Fifth Congress, Second Session—May 4, 1898.

Bureau of Ordnance Newport Torpedo Station: Enlarging storehouse, improvements and repairs to seaman gunners' quarters, and providing more adequate accommodations for the increasing number of torpedo boats sent to the station for outfits and torpedo work, ten thousand five hundred dollars.

Smokeless Powder Factory: For the erection of buildings on government ground for the manufacture of smokeless powder, with the necessary machinery and equipment, ninety-three thousand seven hundred and twenty-seven dollars.

Increase of the Navy: … sixteen torpedo boat destroyers of about four hundred tons displacement, and twelve torpedo boats of about hone hundred and fifty tons displacement, to have the highest practicable speed, and to cost in all, exclusive of armament, not exceeding six million nine hundred thousand dollars; and one gunboat to take the place of the United States steamboat *Michigan.*

And not more than two of said battle ships, and not more than two of said harbor-defense vessels, and not more than five of said torpedo boat destroyers, and not more than four of said torpedo boats shall be built in one yard or by one contracting party.

Fifty-Fifth Congress, Third Session—March 3, 1899.

Bureau of Ordnance: Smokeless Powder Factory, necessary expenses incident to the work of continuing the development of the smokeless powder factory, twenty-five thousand dollars.

Fifty-Sixth Congress, First Session—June 7, 1900.

Increase of the Navy: The Secretary of the Navy, is hereby authorized and directed to contract for five submarine torpedo boats of the Holland type of the most improved design, at a price not to exceed one hundred and seventy thousand dollars each: provided, that such boats shall be similar in dimensions to the proposed new Holland, plans and specifications of which were submitted to the Navy Department by the Holland torpedo Boat Company November twenty-third, eighteen hundred ninety-nine.

The said new contract and the submarine torpedo boats covered by the same are to be in accordance with the stipulations of the contract the Holland Torpedo Boat Company, represented by the Secretary of said company, the party of the first part, and the united States, represented by the Secretary of the Navy, the party of the second part.

Equipment: Toward the completion of the equipment outfit of the new vessels heretofore authorized four hundred thousand dollars.

Fifty-Sixth Congress, Second Session—March 3, 1901.

Public Works—Bureau of Ordnance: Naval Torpedo Station, Newport, Rhode Island; one administration building for use in instruction of classes of enlisted men and officers, to contain offices, lecture rooms, overhauling room, and storeroom for torpedoes, to be immediately available, twenty-five thousand dollars.

Fifty-Seventh Congress, First Session—July 1, 1902.

Public Works—Bureau of Ordnance: Naval Torpedo Station, Newport, Rhode Island: Renewing sea wall on east side of Goat Island, filling in and grading; erection and equipment of a carpenter's shop and one set of quarters, twenty-eight thousand dollars.

Fifty-Seventh Congress, Second Session—March 3, 1903.

Bureau of Ordnance: Purchase and manufacture of smokeless powder, five hundred thousand dollars.

Fifty-Eighth Congress, Second Session—April 27, 1904.

Bureau of Ordnance: Purchase and installation of machine tools at the Torpedo Station, Newport Rhode Island, five thousand dollars. For one chemist, at two thousand five hundred dollars; one clerk at one thousand two hundred dollars; one draftsman at one thousand five hundred dollars. Addition to chemical laboratory, one thousand dollars; addition to seaman's quarters and central latrine for employees, one thousand six hundred dollars; coal shed and shed for fire lose and fire apparatus, one thousand five hundred dollars; fireproof storehouse for torpedo boat supplies, thirty thousand dollars; in all, Newport, Rhode Island, thirty-four thousand one hundred dollars.

Increase of the Navy: The Secretary of the Navy is hereby authorized, in his discretion, to contract for, purchase subsurface, or submarine torpedo boats in the aggregate of, but not exceeding eight hundred and fifty thousand dollars: *Provided*, That prior to said purchase or contract for said boats any American inventor or owner of a subsurface or submarine torpedo boat may give reasonable notice and have his, her, or its subsurface or submarine torpedo boat tested by comparison, together with its recommendations, to the Secretary of the Navy, who may purchase or contract for subsurface or submarine torpedo boats in a manner that will best advance the interests of the United States in torpedo or submarine warfare: *And provided further*, That before any subsurface or submarine torpedo boat is purchased or contracted for it shall be accepted by the Navy Department as fulfilling all reasonable requirements for submarine warfare and shall have been fully tested to the satisfaction of the Secretary of the Navy. To carry out the purpose aforesaid the um of eight hundred and fifty thousand dollars is hereby appropriated out of any money in the treasury not otherwise appropriated; and to make up said sum of eight hundred and fifty thousand dollars, the sum of five hundred thousand dollars carried, or such parts thereof as may remain unexpended, and authorized in the naval appropriation Act, approved March third, nineteen hundred and three, is hereby re-appropriated.

Fifty-Eighth Congress, Third Session—March 3, 1905.

Bureau of Ordnance: Torpedo Station, Newport Rhode Island: For labor, material, freight and express charges; general care of and repairs to grounds, buildings, and wharves, boats, instruction, instruments, tools, furniture, experiments, and general torpedo outfits, sixty-five thousand dollars.

For the purchase of reserve torpedoes and appliances, one hundred thousand dollars.

Fifty-Ninth Congress, First Session—June 29, 1906.

Bureau of Ordnance, Public Works: Torpedo Station, Newport Rhode Island: Repairs to sea wall, five thousand three hundred dollars; extension of tinsmith shop, one thousand eight hundred dollars; new paint shop, one thousand two hundred dollars.

For the purchase or manufacture of reserve torpedoes and appliances, two hundred and fifty thousand dollars: *Provided*, that of this amount not more than one hundred fifty-five dollars shall be used for the construction and equipment of a torpedo factory at the torpedo station at Newport, Rhode Island.

Increase of the Navy: Three torpedo boat destroyers, to have the highest practicable speed, and to cost, exclusive of armament, not to exceed seven hundred and fifty thousand dollars each.

Endnotes

1. For thrilling true-life stories of torpedo boat adventures during the Spanish-American War, see Building the Mosquito Fleet: the U.S. Navy's First Torpedo Boats, Arcadia Publishing, 2001.
2. The Herreshoff brothers, John Brown and Nathanael Greene, originally built the speedy Stiletto as their private yacht in which they won every race they competed.
3. The single fault of the weapon is that its angle of fire was static, which compelled the ship to move so that the guns are pointing at the target.
4. Sources are at odds to Howell's Navy rank during the dates sited that concern his flywheel torpedo.
5. During tests in the Seaconnet River a few Howells were lost when they failed to float to the surface after their run. One of the lost torpedoes was recovered when a fisherman's net snagged it in the late 1970s.The torpedo was brought to the Naval Undersea Warfare Center by the Center's explosive ordnance team. When the torpedo was dismantled, its interior workings were found to be in near-perfect condition; the gyroscope, after being cleaned worked flawlessly.
6. Late in 1917, as the U.S., became deeply involved in the great European war, Washington was concerned with the German submarine threat. It was then an ambitious antisubmarine plan was hatched. The expensive loss of crucial supplies on route to European allies troubled Rear Admiral David W. Taylor, Chief of the Bureau of Construction and Repair, who thought that airplanes should be developed capable of flying across the Atlantic. Transport of large capacity bombers to Europe was dangerous business. Ironically, submarines were sinking cargo vessels carrying aircraft capable of searching and destroying German U-boats. Although production of patrol floatplanes was increasing, deck space and ship's holds were jammed with troops and military hardware. As a solution, the Navy resolved to build flying boats large enough to cross the Atlantic under their own power. Once on friendly European bases, the planes would have sufficient range to hunt and destroy the prowling German submarines. Thus commenced the Navy-Curtiss giant flying boat program—designated NC and using the Navy's ship numbering system.

Bibliography

All referenced titles published by the United States Government Printing Office are available to the public, if currently in stock, by making a request to the Printing Office in Washington, DC or the Public Affairs Office, Naval Undersea Warfare Center, Newport, RI 02840. Other titles listed are currently out of print but may be found on the secondary market.

Note on Sources

The text, photographs, and illustrations for are from diverse sources, the author has made every effort to identify those sources.

Illustrations are from contemporary periodicals, period post cards, and official U.S. Navy photos released for public information. Generally, text is from official, copyright free government documents: articles, brochures, reports, and presentations pertaining to the history of the Naval Torpedo Station and its descendant facilities released for public information; also, mid-to-late nineteenth century commercial books, scientific journals, technical magazines and pamphlets all in the public domain.

A Century of Progress, 1869–1969, Naval Undersea Warfare Center, Newport Division, U.S. Government Printing Office, 1998.

Archibald, Sherman C.; *Newport and The Savings Bank*, A. Hartley G. Ward, Newport, RI, 1944

Centennial Commemoration, Naval Underwater Weapons Research and Engineering Station, Newport, RI, U.S. Government Printing Office, 1969.

Engineering, a weekly British technical tabloid, January 4, 1878

Cowell, Mary Anne; *Newport and Navy Torpedoes - An Enduring Legacy*, (an Internet file)

Gray, Edwyn; *The Devil's Device*, Seeley, Service and Co., Ltd., London, 1975.

Greene, Welcome Arnold; *Providence Plantations for 250 Years*, J. A. & R. A. Reid, Providence, 1886.

Haley, John Williams; *The Old Stone Bank History of Rhode Island*, Vol. IV. Providence Institution for Savings, Providence, RI, 1944.

Heiferman, Ronald; *U.S. Navy in World War II*, Chartwell Books, Inc., Secaucus, NJ, 1978.

Hefferman, John B.; Rear Admiral, U.S.N. (Ret.), "Submarines" in *Encyclopedia Americana* (International Ed.; New York; Americana Corporation, 1970), pp. 766-768; Hall, Richard Compton; *Submarine Boats* (New York, Arco, 1983), pp. 32-44, pp. 92-109, details much of Holland's work, including that for the Navy.

Herreshoff, Grace; 'The U.S. Naval Torpedo Station', *Harper's New Monthly Magazine*, 1902.

Hughes, W. S.; Lieutenant, U.S. Navy, 'Modern Aggressive Torpedoes', *Scribner's Magazine*, Vol. I, January–June, 1887.

Humble, Richard; *History of the United States Navy*, Chevprime Ltd, 1988.

Jolie, H. W.; *A Brief History of U.S. Navy Torpedo Development*, Naval Underwater Systems Center, Technical Document 5436, U.S. Government Printing Office, 15 September, 1978.

Major Scientific and Technological Facilities at NUSC, NUSC Technical Document 6320, U.S. Government Printing Office, 1 March, 1986.

Merrill, John and Lionel D. Wyld; *Meeting the Submarine Challenge,*
U.S. Government Printing Office, 1997.

Mk 13 Aircraft-Launched Torpedo: A World War II Success Story, Naval Undersea Warfare Center Division, NUWC-NPT Technical Document 10,056, U.S. Government Printing Office, 30 July 1992.

Mk 14 Submarine-Launched Torpedo: Four Decades of Service, Naval Undersea Warfare Center Division, NUWC-NPT Technical Document 10,254 U.S. Government Printing Office, 19 April 1994.

Mk 15 Destroyer-Launched Torpedo: End of an Era, Naval Undersea Warfare Center Division, NUWC-NPT Technical Document 10,132, U.S. Government Printing Office, 23 August 1993.

Navy Yearbook, Compilation of Annual Naval Appropriation Laws from 1883 to 1913. U.S. Government Printing Office, 1913.

Nicolosi, Anthony, S.; 'Foundations of the Naval Presence in Narragansett Bay, an Overview', *Bulletin of the Newport Historical Society,* Vol. 52, Part 3, Number 175, Summer 1979.

Panaggio, Leonard J.; *Portrait of Newport,* Mowbray Company, Providence, 1969.

Shafter, Richard A.; *Destroyers in Action,* Cornell Maritime Press, New York, 1945.

Sherman, Archibald C.; *Newport and the Savings Bank,* A. Hartley G. Ward, Newport, 1944.

Simpson, Richard V., *Building the Mosquito Fleet: the U.S. Navy's First Torpedo Boats,* Arcadia Publishing, Charleston, SC, 2001.

———— *Historic Tales of Colonial Rhode Island,* The History Press, Charleston, SC, 2012.

Skerrett, Robert G.; 'The Whitehead Torpedo', *The Technical World,* August 1904, Vol. 1, No. 6, pp. 647-654.

———— *The Torpedoes Full Speed Ahead!,* Naval Torpedo Station, Keyport, Washington, 1976.

Stensrud, Rockwell; *Newport, A Lively Experiment – 1639–1969,* Redwood Library and Athenaeum, Newport, RI, 2006.

'Torpedoes and Torpedo Boats', *Harper's New Monthly Magazine,* 1882, pp. 36-47.

Weapons Systems Department, NUSC Technical Document 6216, U.S. Government Printing Office, 28 September 1984.

About the Author

Richard V. Simpson is a native Rhode Islander who has always lived within walking distance to Narragansett Bay; first in the Edgewood section of Cranston and in Bristol where he has lived since 1960.

A graphic designer by trade, he worked in advertising, printing, display, and textile design studios. He designed and built parade floats for Kaiser Aluminum's Bristol plant and the Navy in Newport; he painted large murals for Kaiser, Raytheon's Submarine Signal Division, and outdoor billboards depicting U.S. Navy Supply Corps history for   the Naval Supply Center in Newport.

After retiring in 1996 from a 29-year Federal Civil Service career with the U.S. Navy Supply Center and Naval Undersea Warfare Center in Newport, he began a second career as an author of books on subjects of historical interest in Rhode Island's East Bay, with his principle focus on Bristol.

This is Richard's twenty-second published title, the second with a military theme as its subject. Beginning in 1985, he acted as contributing editor for the national monthly *Antiques & Collecting Magazine* in which 85 of his articles on antique and collectable subjects have appeared.

Bristol's famous Independence Day celebration and parade was Richard's first venture in writing a major history narrative. His 1989 *Independence Day: How the Day is Celebrated in Bristol, Rhode Island* is the singular authoritative book on the subject; his many anecdotal Fourth of July articles have appeared in the local *Bristol Phoenix* and the *Providence Journal*. His history of Bristol's Independence Day celebration is the source of a story in the July 1989 *Yankee Magazine*, and July 4, 2010 issue of *Parade Magazine*, and an interview on National Public Radio.

Books by Richard V. Simpson

A History of the Italian-Roman Catholic Church in Bristol, RI (1967).
Independence Day: How the Day is Celebrated in Bristol, RI (1989).
Old St. Mary's: Mother Church in Bristol, RI (1994).
Bristol, Rhode Island: In the Mount Hope Lands of King Philip (1996).
Portsmouth, Rhode Island, Pocasset: Ancestral Lands of the Narragansett (1997).
Tiverton and Little Compton, Rhode Island: Pocasset and Sakonnet (1997).
Tiverton and Little Compton, Rhode Island: Volume II (1998).
Bristol, Rhode Island: The Bristol Renaissance (1998).
America's Cup Yachts: The Rhode Island Connection (1999).
Building the Mosquito Fleet: U.S. Navy's First Torpedo Boats (2001).
Bristol: Montaup to Poppasquash (2002).
Bristol, Rhode Island: A Postcard History (2005).
Narragansett Bay: A Postcard History (2005).
Herreshoff Yachts: Seven Generations (2007).
Historic Bristol: Tales from an Old Rhode Island Seaport (2008).
The America's Cup: Trials and Triumphs (2010).
The Quest for the America's Cup: Sailing to Victory (2012).
Tiverton & Little Compton Rhode Island: Historic Tales of the Outer Plantations (2012).
Historic Tales of Colonial Rhode Island: Aquidneck Island and the Founding of the Ocean State (2012).
Preserving Bristol: Restoring, Reviving and Remembering (2014).
Thomas Lipton's America's Cup Campaigns (2014).